FOOTSTEPS
FROM EAST COKER

FOOTSTEPS
FROM EAST COKER

David Foot

FAIRFIELD BOOKS

Fairfield Books
17 George's Road, Bath BA1 6EY
Tel 01225-335813

First published 2010

ISBN 978 0 9560702 7 2

Printed and bound in Great Britain by
Midway Colour Print, Trowbridge, Wiltshire

Contents

Acknowledgements

My especial gratitude goes of course to my beloved East Coker, where first I played cricket and, before that, broadened my education from what I viewed and heard from my bedroom window. I thank the quartet who rashly encouraged me to put this jumble of thoughts and memories into a book – my publisher Stephen Chalke, the editor of *Wisden Almanack* Scyld Berry, fellow journalist and author Ivan Ponting, and son Mark. I'm grateful to local historians like Abigail Shepherd and Gerry Smith and all the others who over the years passed on their impressions and those priceless snippets that I stored away in my head. Mark gave me his photograph of Five Ashes burial ground. I thank all who generously offered me their time for a chat over the garden gate in the shadow of Verandah Cottage. And how can I ignore all those who came to my aid as I tried to cope with an alien and wayward computer?

To my large, loving family, full of fun and lift whenever my confidence was starting to sag a little. They all surely deserve a mention: Anne; Mark and Vivien, Julia and David; Emma and James, Rachel and Lars, twins Clare and Sarah; James and Polly; great grandson Archie

1

FOOTLOOSE

It was, I suppose, a presumptuous starting point. My short story, posted off in a spirit of youthful creative satisfaction, seemed to me to be automatically en route to publication. The quiet confidence sprang from absurd naïvete rather than any tiresome egotistical trait. Within four days the undersized package containing my virgin manuscript had been returned to me, perhaps in those distant days some kind of record for a rejection slip.

Maybe I was ill-prepared for my fledgling literary experience. I was barely eight years old and had sent my superficial psychological tale about what would now be called a geeky young man called Clarence (it is all I can remember) to the then successful and stylish *Strand Magazine*. My contribution had been written in a school exercise book in red ink. It was presented in my best joined-up handwriting, neat and more or less double-spaced. The rejection took me by surprise, not least the insensitive note that the editor or his deputy had impatiently scribbled alongside the ritual stereotyped words that informed me they didn't want to know of Clarence's ingenuous complexes. "Just don't waste our time with rubbish like this. And at least make some effort in presenting it properly," thundered the editorial rebuke. I gazed incredulously at the words that I didn't fully understand. It was a cruel reaction to a lad who didn't yet know how to use a typewriter. Worse, I had sacrificed a stamp for the reply which I imagined would be accompanied by a modest cheque.

That had been in the late thirties. When the *Strand Magazine* closed in 1950 I shed no tears. I had already read by this time that the *Strand*'s contributors had included Graham Greene, Rudyard Kipling, GK Chesterton, Sir Arthur Conan Doyle, Georges Simenon, PG Wodehouse, Somerset Maugham, HG Wells, Max Beerbolm, CB Fry and Edgar Wallace. They make up a formidable literary line-up. Not that any of them would then have made much impression on me, an utterly unworldly eight-year-old whose reading matter was limited, as I propped my weekly comic or grandfather's porridge-stained *News Chronicle* against the paraffin lamp on the kitchen table.

I am not sure that is strictly true. I'd have liked the sounds of some of those names. Doyle would have been familiar to me. Might he have been a relative, I'd have asked myself, of Jimmy Doyle, a loquacious, exotic word-spinning New Scotland Yard exile who was spending his retirement years, telling absorbing tales of criminal deeds as he ran the bar at *The Quiet Woman*, a convivial local in the hamlet of Halstock five miles away from my East Coker home?

A summer or two later, still a boy with short trousers and burgeoning imagination, I returned to my *Strand* team, though I didn't see them in any way as literary figures. In the school holidays I staged my own Test matches, pounding my tennis ball against the crumbling brickwork of our small two-seater lavatory at the top of the garden. The pitch was short and taxingly tortuous; I made my own rules, representing both England and Australia in complicated fashion – documenting every run at the end of my intense delivery.

Somerset Maugham, whom I felt because of his name had some geographical allegiance to my native heath, used to open the batting and topped the averages. It carried the semblance of a creative exercise, certainly not the soulless jottings of an emerging anorak. I wasn't aware of *Wisden* so had no reason to consult its pages as I encountered technical problems on the uneven lavatory track. The rules, followed and occasionally bent as my Test matches progressed, were a constant joy. Criticism came from a domestic source.

My mother, a neat woman in always freshly laundered pinny, didn't really approve of my sporting imaginings as played out under the weary, sap-leaking old yew. "It's not the place to be spending your holidays. Too smelly, David. Why don't you go off and pick some wild flowers for me instead?" Her argument was based on a sense of rural hygiene, allowing no time for any contemplative study of what my top-of-the-garden foraging might reveal as I hunted for a cross-batted on-drive of sorts among nature's drooping dandelions, stinging nettles and a secret insect kingdom inhabited for the moment by the unlikely presence of someone, an emerging sporting hero, called Edgar Wallace.

Mother was right about the smell, of course. Every six months or so, Dad, with the lugubrious earthy humour of a Shakespearean gravedigger, would clear the accumulated family faeces and deposit them in the vegetable garden to the evident benefit of the parsnips, turnips and the other root crops. It was a ritual he didn't much enjoy but, well, it had to be done. What was a wheelbarrow for? Life for a few months became less rewarding for the bumble bees whose droning chorus disappeared overnight. I had little sympathy for them. When in midsummer our two-seater was actively open for business, those obese and boringly melodious bees caused me great consternation with their flirtatious frolics, disconcertingly out of sight, as they went on their sorties in the direction of my unprotected genitals.

This was especially disturbing in the late evenings; our small lavatory may have boasted two well-scrubbed functional seats but like the whole of the cottage it had no lighting. Nature's spooky summons demanded that we carried a rusty torch, the lav lamp. Constipation lengthened the stay and was not to be encouraged. Cottage dwellers at my home village, most of them working on local farms or the twine factory for a pittance, didn't indulge in the purchase of toilet rolls. We pragmatically used sheets of newspapers instead, and I remember that I worried incessantly about whether whole columns of printers' ink would be transferred to my fleshy bottom.

Oddly my make-believe cricket, in no way yet inhibited by *Wisden*'s biblical tablets of guidance, did not involve the use of a bat. Runs were determined by the deviations, pace and weed-strewn route as my tennis ball rebounded off the privy's undulating brickwork. I used to come in off a short, staccato run and often missed the ball as it came back off the wall, gathering muscle and mischief as it did so. Never acknowledging sluggish fielding, I paused only to document four runs in my improvised scorebook, perched prominently against the adjacent chicken run.

This, I suppose, was my cherished introduction to cricket. It has remained unchallenged in my sporting affections ever since, despite the demeaning one-day side shows, the necessary new repertoire of shots, and the new language that players now use. I have no intention to bemoan cricket's extraordinary evolution, at times exciting as well as over-congested and of course plentifully supported. There was a good deal that I once disliked socially, but now I am apt to fidget in confusion. It's another game altogether. An incorrigible romantic, I miss too much. It was for me more of a delight alongside the chicken run – Rhode Island Reds and PG Wodehouse on the boundary, leaning against the wire netting.

We lived in a Virginia creeper-clad cottage opposite the village pub, then known as the *New Inn* and now the *Helyar Arms*. On Saturday nights, I would safely wedge myself in the lower branches of a mountain ash tree and wait for a few of the cricket team to cycle home from the match. The discoloured pads would be strapped to their cross-bars; their demeanours usually reflected whether East Coker CC had won. By now I actually realised that eleven disparate exponents from the pages of current literature didn't make up a cricket team. Instead 'Tammy' Neville was employed at the twine works and didn't open the bowling for Somerset. Johnnie Stevens, a naturally talented cricketer, was more likely to be heard singing in the church choir than bawling an lbw appeal. As yet, I was unaware of the names of any county players. In retrospect, that was a pity.

Bill Andrews, soon to be taken on briefly by the lord of the manor as the village pro – who cut the grass at the local ground and helped some of the more talented lads with the coaching – was staying at the pub. Bill was one of the most popular players to represent Somerset, even if he was sacked four times and offered without being asked unequivocal views on most subjects, guaranteed to upset the county's starchy establishment. He had a memorable stay at the *New Inn*, where his terrier was a constant companion and where Bill's thirst was manfully prodigious. Before long he was on his way to Taunton where he twice completed the double and reckoned that only Wally Hammond had blocked his ascent towards a Test cap.

Bill, with all his endearing vocal excesses, had the warmest of hearts. For years he was an imperishable hero of mine. He was a patient and good-natured tutor and taught me how to refine my off-break. (Mind you, he had so much self-confidence that he probably offered the same advice to Jim Laker.) His wife, Ennyd, had the secret for the best home-made wine in the West Country. The Surrey side celebrated with it in goodly measure after they had won another championship pennant in the 1950s, Bill arriving in glowing and impartial mood from his Weston-super-Mare home with bottles of it.

Several years before, when I was working for a weekly paper on the Somerset-Dorset border, worshipping the lofty Andrews mostly from the published match reports, one of my duties as secretary of the village XI was to find a speaker for our annual dinner. I wrote to Bill. To the delight of my team-mates he accepted. So far, so good. But the dinner was being held in a local hotel, on a Friday. Alas, it was also market day in Yeovil; the licensing hours were extended. He arrived early and generously sampled the ales. By the time he reached our hotel, the dining room reverberated to the booming, jolly sounds of his voice. The distinctive stammer was still there. So were the countless stories of his contemporaries. It was said he had a story about every one of them, a little fictitious in the telling maybe but never worse than mildly slanderous.

Most of the boys in my village club had not met a county cricketer before. They plied Bill with pints.

"Now tell us, Mr Andrews, about your mate Arthur Wellard." He would have talked all night about his idol and closest friend.

"You want to hear about Arthur, then. Best all-rounder Somerset ever had."

"And was it true, em, Arthur could remember the order of every card in the pack?"

It was 'Arthur' all round by this time.

"That's right," Andrews confirmed. "No-one could touch him at poker, either, or when we all rushed off with him after the closing overs for an evening race meeting."

The rosy-cheeked, rotund players of East Coker CC wanted more. Bill told them of the fancy shoes with pointed toes that Wellard used to wear, the flashy sports coats, the hair-style that Andrews admitted he used to copy.

And then suddenly, as a gust of wind swept through the hotel, the flushed and amiable William Harry Russell Andrews vigorously rubbed his fingers and announced to no-one in particular: "It's getting bloody cold – why haven't they lit the fire in here?" In the same movement, he pulled a box of matches from his pocket, stooped and lit the meticulously aligned paper in the grate.

What Bill had failed to note was that it was an artificial fireplace. The paper caught light immediately, along with the other contents. Very soon the dining room was engulfed in smoke. The assembled company made for the door, spluttering in their beer. Hotel staff struggled to cover the bread rolls. The flames were extinguished and everything returned to normal. We sat down for our meal an hour later than scheduled, although no-one seemed too bothered. Bill went on with his stories; it gave him time for a couple more pints before the meal.

But I am racing ahead. I must return to the pre-Andrews days when I walked the mile home from the village school in little brown jersey and matching tie that my mother had knitted for me. We were a family which didn't talk much, never about cricket as far as I remember. The silences were long as we sat round the kitchen table; they still conveyed that we were comfortable in our unspoken rapport. When Dad would occasionally stretch to switch on the cumbersome wireless, large, heavy and disproportionate in size within a cottage dwelling, Mother retained an expression of mild disapproval. In her entrenched working-class code of conduct, distractions like the Jack Payne orchestra were not to be encouraged during meal-time.

The lack of conversation in village homes, especially then, was commonplace. I have never quite escaped its restrictions, and it is one of the reasons that I became more of a listener in what should have been animated sporting duologues. In truth, it served me equally well in what was to be my chosen career. In the 1930s I don't recall a single mention of domestic praise for Hobbs and Hammond, although my family dutifully passed on their potted biographies of such distinguished cricketers from the backs of the cigarette cards.

"Don't think you've got this bloke, David," my father said, dangling a Woodbine between his lips. "Thanks, Dad." And that was it.

Cricket, however, stirred me like few other facets of my young life. My parents were in their way oddly protective. For a reason I never quite comprehended, they didn't like me to wander off to the other end of the village. Maybe they thought I would lose myself among unfamiliar households. It is also possible that because our side of East Coker housed the Norman church, it psychologically offered an aura of guardianship. But from time to time in the summer months I would dream up an ingenious fiction to satisfy my parents, enabling me to chase away, up and down Tellis Hill and past the school to the cricket pitch. By then Bill Andrews had gone, passing the duties of cutting the outfield and chasing off Farmer Denning's sheep to brother Jack. I used to go by stealth on rare Saturday afternoons and sit cross-legged on the boundary. That, I imagined, was what it was like to watch a Test match.

East Coker cricket team, two years before I was born

Consciously I didn't position myself too far from the little pavilion. I'd gaze at the iridescent caps of players who clearly pretended they were still playing for their schools. Some of them talked with posh accents. I noticed that they stayed in little incestuous groups away from the village lads. Such divisions didn't then so much bother me; I was too young after all to question the social order. The polemics would come years later. For the time being I was content to eavesdrop as the humbler players from the parish, in the team on merit, wandered past me, never wholly satisfied about their lowly place in the batting order. I suspected that they had a genuine grievance.

I liked to see Tom Hackwell in the side. They used to joke that he knew a thing or two about the quality of the willows. So he should have. The slightly gloom-laden Tom, who had a sort of incongruous Charlie Chaplin moustache, was the village undertaker; he worked all the time in wood. His workshop was only just down the road from the pitch. When trade was brisk, his array of partially fashioned coffins were on public view as you walked past. The brass handles glinted in the sunlight. There couldn't have been a more frightening symbolic sign for fledgling players as they approached the ground, pondering their fate against uncoordinated fast bowlers with flailing, hairy arms and unsubtle intentions.

Herbert Dodge was another eye-catching member of the side. He was a tall, serious man with a bearing and voice in keeping with his professional occupation. He was renowned for one specific stroke which allowed the ball to travel under his deliberately raised left pad on its predetermined journey towards the fine leg boundary. The highly specialised shot was expected of him and was duly greeted by collective chortles from his approving team-mates.

From my cross-legged, solitary vantage point in my own uncomplicated world, I acquired favourites among the local lads. I knew their jobs if not their names. One was a stockbroker though I didn't know what that entailed. Another had a milk round – and a young son who to my surprise some years later would become a Tory MP.

And then there was the teenage Ken Gillingham, whose background I never quite discovered. What I did feel was that he was a diffident opening batsman of distinct style. It was his walk to the wicket that held my attention. He had a slender figure; he didn't move with the less graceful deportment of a village boy, though that I am sure was what he was. He would, I told myself, be opening for Somerset one day. Sadly he didn't get that far. His name, as a gunner in the Royal Artillery, is carved alongside too many others from East Coker who gave their lives during the two World Wars. Charlie Mayo was another. After leaving Eton he played club cricket with skill and enthusiasm, as well as six times for his county.

Why did he die a modest sergeant? So many questions remain unanswered. I always assumed he was a young man of some independent means, a good-looking bachelor. He lived opposite me in the village, in a handsome house with a gravelled drive – then a recognition of status – and a large manicured rear lawn. Perhaps noticing my shyness, he would encourage me to talk cricket with him as we leaned over my garden gate. Charlie had a pet raven which accompanied him on many of his strolls through the village lanes. Years later I was solemnly told that the raven met a premature end, hastened – I conclude – by the action of the constabulary. The trouble was that the raven apparently developed some tendencies to sexual fetishism. It routinely visited all the washing lines, purloining ladies' knickers. And with salacious discrimination, the raven limited its patrolling peccadillo sorties to the frilly undies of female gender. The bird was utterly unashamed, brazen even, in its perversions.

I don't believe the raven ever accompanied Charlie to a cricket match. It is possible that the players' wives and girl friends in their summer dresses were seen as too much of a risk. But cricket, like no other game, has for ever been a treasury for colourful margin notes and delicious peripheral absurdities. I have always been willingly ensnared, at times against my nature, by the game's whims and corny rituals as well as the oddball people it has attracted. Some have disappeared, squeezed out by frenetic fixture lists, a surfeit of new global competitions, impersonal and soulless attitudes and a madcap, even more suffocating plutocracy.

My affection remains, even if a little less steadfast. It continues to seduce me at the highest Ashes level, just as it once did in early evening between the cowpats in a buttercup meadow. Somewhere in between, cricket has lost its character and joyful purpose – and I don't much like it.

Let me go back again to my early schooldays. Did the mere notion of cricket really dominate my sporting affections? The whiff of linseed oil left my nostrils reluctantly. But I fancy there was also a place, however nebulous and superficial, for horse-racing and specifically the Grand National. It was a colourful, romantic pursuit I shared with Yvonne, who was two or three years younger and lived next door. We competed at Aintree together and I suppose, in the sweetest and most innocent of liaisons, she was my first girl friend. My father's vegetable garden was a big one, with narrow paths and small apple trees – like the locally named Coker Seedling – that provided their own hazards. I would lay Dad's hoes and forks across the paths, marginally lifted off the ground, to provide the illusion of jumps amid the pretence of such equine grandeur. Selfishly I was always Golden Miller, that wondrous thoroughbred of his day. The course may not have been four miles long but it was still a taxing test of unconventional horsemanship. Vonnie, my next-door playmate, was game in stamina over the jumps and diligent in taking instruction from the Clerk of the Course. We would prepare for the big race with a succession of early-morning gallops (as soon as my father had gone to work). And we took the National seriously. With a sense of exaggerated drama I usually contrived to fall at Beecher's. It was as realistic as I could make it.

The race, which lacked only the big crowds and the raucous competing inducements of the bookies, was – I suppose – a feat of imagination. There was dew on the ground when I conscientiously walked the course with a rake in pre-National homage. Just once I had heard a fragment of the race on the family wireless, while a glance at my grandfather's *Chronicle* offered a more graphic image. The rest was in my head.

Football wasn't ignored completely. It was part of working-class culture, with its measure of spontaneous theatre and biased banter. Yeovil & Petters United (later Yeovil Town) were my local semi-pro team. Dad took me to watch them. We went the four miles on the bus and I can still remember the winding little urban short-cuts that took us to the ground. I was entranced by the green shirts of the players and the seemingly obligatory cigars of the well-fleshed directors, mostly from the local gloving industry, in their quaint little box built on stilts that to me looked in imminent danger of collapsing. We sat on improvised wooden seats not far from the touchline. Curious as ever, I studied the boots the players wore, the emerald and white hooped socks – doubtless knitted by one or two of the wives. I was a little shocked to hear some of the exchanges of warring opponents. Dad, uneasy at the way I found myself extending my still prudish vocabulary, said nothing and hoped I had misheard.

The Huish ground, renowned for its epic Cup wins, was of famous Alpine proportions and wingers had at times to excel as sprinters to keep the ball in play as it gathered pace down the hill. Smells were inclined to make an impression on me. I sniffed the embrocation as players challenged near to my touchline. And the hops from the adjacent Bruttons brewery hovered in hospitable mood over the ground.

During the interval, encouraged by my father, I made my investment for the Penny-on-the-Ball competition. The halftime results, chalked on a blackboard, were also passed round the ground by a supporter with a fussy air of self-importance. There was so much to see. Just like I had pretended my village cricket ground was Lord's, this one was Wembley. I've no idea whether it was a good game. Yeovil won with not much to spare. At the final whistle it seemed that we were all allowed to walk across the field and chat to the nearest player. Dad, who knew plenty about nature and grass-seeding, dug his feet into the ground and said: "Standing up pretty well with all the rain we've had." I can recall his exact words – just as I can the few the Yeovil goalkeeper, Tommy Lynch, had in broad Scottish with a group of enthusing fans. "Great win, that – aye!" I'm not sure it was but it remains one of the greatest games of football I ever saw.

And I can still see Lynch making his saves. He used to stand distinctively, both arms fully outstretched, and I couldn't imagine the likelihood of the ball ever finding a minute gap through which it might possibly squeeze its way into the net. Whenever, years later, I was asked who was the most agile keeper I ever saw, I conveniently ignored Gordon Banks or any of the more glamorous players from the top divisions. "Tommy Lynch," I would reply without hesitation. My conviction also carried a ring of familiarity that was hardly justified on the strength of seeing him only once in action.

Yet I must have been excessively opinionated as a small schoolboy analyst. If Lynch was usually nominated as my number one, Cockles Stevens ran him close. Cockles, or Hubert if we were opting for a more dignified moniker, lived in East Coker where he played for both the village cricket and football teams. It was his thick yellow goalkeeper's jersey that I could still visually recapture for ages. He excelled, it must be admitted, not so much for any balletic leaps as for the sheer distance he could kick the ball. His goalkicks landed not far from the opposing penalty area, or beyond. Like cricketer Johnnie Stevens (same family), he had a regular Sunday date at the parish church of St Michael's. He possessed a powerful baritone voice which was used effectively as he read the lesson for matins or evensong. Powers of concentration were never a strong point of mine. Whenever I saw him striding up to the lectern, I remembered again those prodigious kicks – and thought I'd rather see him in his yellow jersey than that freshly starched surplice.

It never seemed quite fair that my own goalkeeping heroes failed to earn the accolade of cigarette-card recognition. Through many a winter's evening, after the supper things had been put away, I would nestle nearer to the oil lamp and affectionately lay out my cards in meticulous rows, reprimanding myself if Norma Shearer or Deanna Durbin, even the ubiquitous Derek McCulloch – *Children's Hour*'s Uncle Mac – had strayed from another pile. I had several albums of footballers, issued by WD & HO Wills. Again it was the variety of team shirts that mesmerised me. Motherwell, as modelled by John McMenemy, and Norwich City, canary-influenced in the upper shirt pattern of EJ Vinall, their one-time centre-forward 'whose shooting was excellent', in particular hypnotised me.

I was struck by the fact that the majority of the players featured in the album had seemingly taken infinite pains over their hair styles. The centre partings had been painstakingly measured, some slammed back, one supposes, with sweet-smelling brilliantine after the latest visit to the barber's. The card of Aberdeen's William Mills made him look like a choirboy; Sunderland's Horatio Carter had the authoritarian sternness of a potential JP.

Eddie Hapgood was in my set entirely on merit, as Arsenal and England's captain. I had no idea then, however, that he was a Bristolian whose early and brief history with the Rovers carried a less than riveting opportunity for him to lug sacks of coal on his shoulders in the summer months to boost his meagre pocket money. There was also Ted Drake, a tenacious, fearless international, always being battered by beefy centre halves lacking any sense of basic chivalry. Fifty years later I pulled out that crumpled cigarette card after my childlike honour of being invited to play alongside him in a cricket benefit match in a Somerset village. Ted was of course a good enough cricketer to play for Hampshire. We sat next to each other in the little pavilion and what I noticed was his impeccably ironed kit. Old pros took this characteristic pleasure in their appearance. But in the pre-war era, I didn't really know too much about him, apart from his imperishable feat of scoring all seven goals for Arsenal against Aston Villa and that his London ground, Highbury, shimmered with glamour.

So, if a little less evident than East Coker's cricket pitch, did the adjoining football ground with its all-purpose dressing room of peeling woodwork and rusty defiance. If the place needed a lick of paint, I didn't see it.

During the winter Saturdays, there was no personal ritual more eagerly awaited than the broadcasting of the football results. The BBC voice, perfectly enunciated, lacked warmth; he could have been relaying a State funeral. But I was happy to augment such dreary one-toned narrative on the radio with all the light and shade from my feverish imagination. It was a duty done in duplicate. Dad had the morning paper; his lead pencil was poised as the results came over the ether. I sat alongside him, excited and anxious. We had only one newspaper so I'd carefully copied in advance every league fixture into a school exercise book. In unison we took down the results, offering our own sparing commentary as the surprises multiplied. "Bloody Barrow, winning at home when you don't want 'em to. Can't usually kick a rice pudding." And Dad so seldom swore when I was around.

My father did the pools, the four aways. He misguidedly thought that one day a fortune might be heading his way. Just once his four aways came up. At least half a dozen times he checked his Littlewoods coupon against the results. Then he checked with me. There was much excitement, maybe secret hopes that his days as an estate worker might be over. And, a few days later, the winnings arrived. They amounted to four shillings. Dad handled the postal order in a mood of abject dismay. We both knew, without saying it aloud, that we would be back optimistically taking down the results again on the following Saturday.

In those distant, dream-laden days, Dad and I documented and fantasised in tandem. I remember it clearly as a regular 1930s talking point in the village. My father would be seen dropping his coupon into the post-box. "Lucky again this week then, Frank?"

"No! It's them northern clubs. Can't rely on 'em. Let me down every time." He was a simple man of few prejudices. Those he possessed seemed to be harmlessly confined to a Littlewoods football coupon.

In some ways he was a demanding taskmaster. He was the church sexton and part of his duties was to try to keep the old building warm. But the heating system, like that in most of the rural churches – where the clergy's stipend was a pittance and the balance sheets were penned by icy fingers – was primitive. On Saturday afternoons I was expected to accompany my father to the improvised subterranean stokehold at the back of the church. As fast as he shovelled in the coke, using the bellows when the paraffin-soaked rolls of newspaper showed a cussed reluctance to ignite in the furnace, I staggered down the steps with countless buckets of fuel.

It was a job I didn't enjoy. Each time I emerged into the pure south Somerset air in search of the next supply of coke, I heard the shouts and cheers wafting all the way from the other end of the village. Coker were at home and I wanted only to know how they were doing. Just occasionally, the yearning in my boyish eyes was impossible to hide and I was allowed to go. By then the fire would be roaring well and I felt I had built up a big enough reserve down in the stokehold to last for the whole season. Before my father had changed his mind I would start running between the stooping tombstones and often didn't stop till I got to the ground. If I was lucky, I'd then see the last half-hour.

Sometimes, not too often, Coker won. On those days, I would cheer and pretend I had seen the whole match. My hands were black with coal dust, my heart throbbing with native pride. And I loved to listen to the conversation as the weary, joyful, unfit players limped off to their tin baths in the dressing room. "Dirty lot of sods, them Bradford Abbas. See the way Nobby Clark was bundled into his own net for their goal? Winger they called Harry should have been sent off for that. Yea, dirty little sod."

I kept quiet. Coker had won. No-one need know that Harry was a cousin of mine.

At the garden gate: my parents and me

2

ELIOT'S EAST COKER

In the late 1930s TS Eliot made his only visits to East Coker, two or three at the most. His ancestors had come from there and it is where his ashes are now buried. He travelled to Yeovil by train and then took a taxi to the Somerset village on the Dorset boundary, imbued as it is with the images and terrain of Thomas Hardy. For one of his returns to Yeovil, he walked down the hill from the parish church, past the Tudor almshouses, to catch Mr Bath's quaint ever-rattling little bus. Timeless transport fitted his pattern and needs.

East Coker Tudor almshouses

He was an observant man. He loved the way the winding lanes were carved out of the sandstone, the high protective roadside hedgerows, the silent miles in which the all-knowing trees outnumbered the houses. His head was full of reflective words as he gazed out of the windows of the old bus: 'Now the light falls across the open field, leaving the deep lane shuttered with branches, dark in the afternoon ...'

Eliot barely knew East Coker but he needed to familiarise himself again with its physical presence and its history. Here around him were the raw materials: all that woodland with the trees ceaselessly murmuring to each other in the gentle wind, the scented wisteria and thatched cottages upon which he could superimpose his abstract thoughts as he wandered his chosen metaphysical by-ways. Ever since those journeys of his, academics have argued and agonised over his elusive meanings. *East Coker*, one of the *Four Quartets*, was published on Good Friday 1940. Countless lectures and tutorials are still devoted to its abstruse brilliance.

The poet himself was a paradox. He liked to be seen as an anonymous figure, never remotely a literary celebrity. Yet he took pains over his appearance, neat and formal as it was. Some saw him as priggish and aloof, pedantically precise in the way he phrased his letters or conducted his conversations. To the surprise of his friends he could emerge with bawdy badinage at dinner parties. He saved his scatological excesses for notes and written exchanges with his special chums. It was as if he was releasing himself from the more familiar strictures of churchgoing and dignified office behaviour.

He was inclined to be snobbish and many claimed he was bigoted. It is true to say he gave the humble, insular village of East Coker acclaim and literary status. Not so many parishes have had a long poem written about them. There is an Eliot Corner in St Michael's Church. Visitors from all over the world come to sit in one of the pews, once more reading his rhythmic and profound verses for hidden links.

I'm not sure what the villagers make of all the fuss. They are proud that he has brought them fame. They accept that he must be exceptional because his name – and East Coker's – is always being mentioned on the radio during serious discussions about Men of Letters. And the list of biographies grows. In the late thirties he walked around the open fields and the farmhouses. There may have been a token "Good afternoon" but no-one would have known who he was. Why should they have? His well-cut suit and expensive trilby may have been a matter of curiosity and warranted a second glance. But, well, he was perhaps 'one of they toffs' who stayed at Coker Court for a few days as house guests.

We didn't go in for too much poetry in the village. On the days of Eliot's visits to the parish church I may have been helping my dad in one of his duties as sexton. I can, however, claim no personal contact with him as, self-consciously I imagine, he strolled into the building one summer's evening and, initially without a word, took up a position behind the ancient font. 'The old man' (vicar) told Dad that someone had come to take a look at the church: "Not sure who he was but he thought he said he was some kind of writer. The name Elliott or something like that was mentioned." There was no name left in the visitors' book; if there had been, I fancy we should have seen only one L and one T. Various spellings of the surname of TS and his ancestors were discovered in the church records.

East Coker church

I don't think there is much doubt about the identity of the solitary member of the congregation that evening. Dad was vague about the direction of the conversation over five or ten minutes at the most. He was halfway up a wooden ladder trimming the wicks of the hanging oil lamps, not so far from the font. "Seemed a nice sort of bloke. Bit religious, too – you could tell that … We had a word about Yeovil & Petters." More likely, it was my father who had a word about Yeovil & Petters, the semi-pro side of modest talent which played in the Southern League. He would have run through the whole team, nick-names and all, as he finished the trimming and topped up the lamp with paraffin. It is hard to think that Eliot shared this intimate knowledge of small-town Saturday aspirations. But he would have politely affected to listen. It should be remembered that my father was a sociable man. He would rub the back of his earthy gardener's hand across his moustache and go up to any church visitors for a chat.

He'd tell them that he had been married in this church, was a sidesman who took the collection once a month and was one of the bell-ringers. Dad might give the Norman pillars a mention in passing, though he wasn't so hot on St Michael's other architectural treasures. He might slip in, too, that he'd been winding the clock by hand for years. No need for false modesty. If the legs were willing and the church visitors appeared in reasonable physical condition, he would offer the favoured parties a peep from the top of the tower. His chummy words weren't wasted. He received dozens of letters, from America and Japan in particular, thanking him for his considerate if potted history.

As a village, albeit a lovely, cosy one already praised by JB Priestley in print, East Coker blissfully was never stifled by notions of self-importance. In those days it refused to bask in Eliot's growing grandeur.

Forty years later I was doing a broadcast on the changing rural scene. A number of the interviews were being done in the village hall at East Coker. It seemed a good moment to slip TS Eliot into the discursive, good-natured narrative. I picked on a stranger and asked him what he thought about having a whole poem named after the parish. "You mean this Eliot feller. Don't think much of his stuff. Bugger me – it don't even rhyme!" I pondered a long time and then rather reluctantly edited that countryman's spontaneous comment out of my piece.

I don't suppose my grandfather made much of it, either. In his way he was an educated man. But his scholarship came from nature. Many of the new generation of sturdy oaks and ashes then, like those on the way to Pincushion Corner, were planted and tended by him. That sylvan statement was his legacy. He struggled to read and write but like so many villagers was appealingly articulate as he talked of the hills and meadows he had known all his life. On Sundays he brought out the big and treasured Bible and read it ponderously with reverential ritual. He said it took him three years to get to the last page, though I am sure it was longer than that. I would go across the road – he lived opposite us – just to watch him and admire his feat of self-discipline. I can still see him moving his grimy nails along each line at painful pace. From time to time he would pause as if to absorb a phrase of spiritual significance. This old gamekeeper was at the same time teaching himself to read. I could not imagine a more inspiring example of true rural academia.

Jack Foot had once been a natural athlete who won races at the local fetes and regularly ran 18 miles each way, after a full day's heavy manual work at Upcerne, to see his wife-to-be Sarah, in service at Sherborne Castle. Now in his kindly rough-and-ready manner he looked after her. For more than 30 years she suffered chronically with arthritis. In the morning he put her across his shoulders, carrying her down the winding, awkward stairway to her permanent seat by the fire. She had a sweet nature and never complained. The doctor was hardly ever summoned although she was no more eventually than a bundle of bones. "Go out in the garden and get me some more nettles, Jack." He would return with a handful of toxic stringing nettles which she immediately rubbed up and down her bony, fragile arms. The theory, passed on by a visiting relative of witchcraft persuasions, was that one pain would offset the other. Jack and Sarah lived in a sparsely furnished cottage, where Jack showed no more than a nominal regard for keeping the living room tidy. One of my jobs was to walk the few hundred yards each Friday to Mrs Ray's miniscule shop. He would dictate what was needed – a packet of Quaker Oats, which seemed to be the staple diet, three pennyworth of extra strong mints and a few boiled sweets, half a dozen candles and an ounce of baccy. Mrs Ray, who would have done well to show any kind of profit on her weekly takings, had a strange repertoire of stock – small tins of salmon, boot polish, cheddar cheese that occasionally looked as though it had seen better days, dog-eared postcards and religious texts. They were all half-displayed in a retail jumble. But Mrs Ray, a small dumpy woman bereft of humour or any talkative trait, appeared miraculously to know the whereabouts of the little shop's varied contents. She supplied my grandfather's basic needs while I was none too concerned as a small boy at any suspect sense of hygiene or disconcerting blend of flavours as the cheese and the peppermints were scooped, unwrapped, into the same white paper bag.

I found her a bit of a misery, possibly an unfair impression. She, it must be admitted, was suspicious of my intentions. There was the time when, influenced by my father's obvious enjoyment of a Woodbine as he dug the garden, I planned my own subterfuge tobacco experiment. I was aware that she sold packets of cheap fags, five for tuppence. It was a price range that I could stand. The daring ruse of handing over two sweaty coins and making my unconvincing illegal purchase was altogether more difficult. I quaked as I stammered my request, saying that it was for my father. She clearly didn't believe me and followed me out of the shop. I ran all the way home, fearful of the consequences. Just once I looked back – and Mrs Ray was still in the roadway, gazing intently at me. I never did taste the tobacco from my virgin drag; instead I took the small, wicked packet of five and hid them, amid mounting guilt, in the pealing bark of one of our apple trees. My self-imposed dare came to nothing. Nor, blissfully, did Mrs Ray's unspoken reprimand. Frankly I don't think she ever forgave me for trying so clumsily to outwit her.

She came to church for Sunday evensong, usually in the same pew near the front. I always felt her piercing, weary eyes were focused on me. It took me years to escape completely from what I saw as that judicial rebuke. Yet my grandfather was a weekly customer, surely not to be turned away, however scant was the profit from his extra strongs or the pre-Christmas quarter of humbugs.

My 'grandfie', as I invariably called him, was a hero of mine. He was well built and manly. He had a thick moustache like Joe Stalin and used to confide to me that he liked "this Russian bloke". Certainly he was not aware of the Communist leader's evil political intentions or contempt for human life. Nor could he understand why everyone was so suspicious of him. That avuncular façade appealed to my grandfather. "Nothing too much wrong with he." For a time I began to think so, too.

In the domestic sense, my grandfather was adept at taking charge. There was the calamitous pitch-black night when my mother was thought to have lost the heavy front-door key. The search began at half past nine after I had returned with my parents from a Sunday service. We were still looking for the key, in various states of panic, mutual accusation and bad temper at midnight. The village was in darkness. There was no space in that small, muddled, two-roomed cottage across the road for any additional occupant to find a stop-gap bed for the night. I was stranded with my parents. An element of despair was turning into a frightening experience, as the night got colder and the missing key, our only one, showed no sign of being discovered.

Grandfather took over. He retrieved a rusty old lantern from the garden shed and lit it. Like ghostly figures, uncertain what to do or where to look, we yet again retraced our steps up and down the church path. And just before 3 a.m. the iron key was spotted in the leaf-strewn drive in front of the silent almshouses. It had been by far the most disturbing high point of drama in my young life. For years it continued to resurface, making me uneasy. The experience had been one of a spooky black emptiness – with no obvious prospect that dawn would eventually arrive. There were just the four of us shuffling around in the crunching gravel, not knowing what to do next. I don't think I am exaggerating in likening the whole, horrid search to that of a small disparate group of blind refugees pleading, without a shared or spoken word, for any semblance of a clue to give them hope and a door to open for shelter. At this distance, in more adult and sophisticated times, I can look back on the scene with the hint of a smile. But for too long it had nagged me as a night of unrelieved blackness and uncertainty that looked as though it would never end.

There should be one final observation on old Jack Foot. He liked a drink, at least when he could afford one. His thirst was proudly paraded on Boxing Day and the other occasions when the local gentry organised their shooting parties. He was recruited as a beater, employed to persuade the game birds to break cover and to chance their luck against the line of twelve-bores. If the occupants from the Big Houses were in a good mood, heartened by their day's booty, Jack would be given half a sovereign, generous reward compared with his painfully modest wages.

He was allowed few days off. But half a sovereign for his back pocket was a bonus not to be wasted. His return home, maybe by way of Hardington, where there were two pubs and always some decent cider, was an extended recreation. Country drinkers seldom mixed their cider with their ale. Jack was an exception. His capacity for strong drink, on those rare days when coins were rattling seductively, knew no bounds. He drank then with an indiscriminate enthusiasm. And that was invariably the case after he had been 'beating' for the squire. He would stay in the bar till his money ran out. "Then his dog would see him home," was a popular verdict in the Coker community. His succession of gun dogs were expertly trained in the manner they retrieved the partridges – and in their faithful duties as they led their staggering gamekeeper back to where Sarah, his gentle wife, waited forbearingly with no more than a shrug as she pulled the shawl more tightly across her shoulders and fragile frame. She was always cold and when he was out, Jack left her a long iron poker to stir and rearrange the apple wood in the fire.

Working-class life was as sexist in Somerset's villages as in the big country houses where the lord of the manor often bellowed the orders, determined the menu and gruffly upbraided the harassed butler. Jack Foot cared for his wife no more and no less than rural custom demanded. His commitment, once he'd brought Sarah down the rickety stairs and eased her into her cushions, was over. I loved them both but I honestly never heard them in conversation. Only in retrospect do I realise how lonely and meaningless life must have been for Sarah. She came from unflinching non-conformist stock and maybe her Methodism helped

I walked alongside her husband for the brief funeral service a quarter of a mile from where they then lived, in the almshouses. It must have been quite a strain for Jack going up Tellis Hill – on the way to the cemetery. At one point he paused, took a cigarette out of his pocket and lit up. There was consternation among the non-conformist contingent. "Here, look at Jack. What does he think he's doing on the way to Sarah's burial?" I knew exactly he was doing. He had just lost his wife – and whatever was irreligious anyway about having a relaxing drag on Tellis Hill? I hated the pious humbug being directed at him.

My grandfather was kept away from the guns on those organised shoots. He was a fine shot and would no doubt have stolen too much of the glory. I was given all the evidence I needed of his shooting skills in his back garden and again seated in front of the fire. He was occasionally lent an air gun and would take me into a position, half-hidden, among his apple trees. Before long the young, melodic sparrows, not so long hatched, would emerge to perch in joyful innocence on the lower branches. Jack made no effort to pop them off. Sitting targets were ignored as part of his countryside code. Instead he waited till a gawky jackdaw fluttered noisily into a higher branch. Instantly the airgun was nestled into the right shoulder. The bird fell to a single pellet, dropping at my feet. "He didn't suffer. Chuck him in the hedge." A lightweight airgun, an over-adventurous jackdaw and an expert shot momentarily excited me. I was still too young to ponder the morality of this back-garden deed of death at the expense of a bird whose only felony was to peck a few onion seeds out of the ground. A few years later, my grandfather's act of mild aggression would have bothered me.

As for his unerring accuracy in the fireplace, I have to admit to a timeless fascination. He'd sit in his armchair, reading the Bible or filling his battered pipe with cheap shag. Irrespective of any passing company, like the doctor on one of his very rare visits, Jack sometimes felt in need of a spit. There were no restrained niceties about it. From a distance of four or five feet, he aimed for the flame. His compounded phlegm hurtled between the bars before sizzling away on a hunk of beech. It was all so perfunctory, so efficient, so hygienic even as the germs were incinerated. The marvel was that, as far as I could see, he never once hit one of the grimy bars as the missive completed its short fatal journey. And in almost the same movement he was back, pressing the odious shag into the bowels of his pipe.

That was Jack and Sarah. Their marriage, despite deprivations, different modes of existence and ill health, lasted a long time. So did that of my parents. The genes served them well.

My mother Margaret grew up in the old mill at Trent, a small village between Yeovil and Sherborne. She began a dressmaking apprenticeship after leaving school but after a road accident went into service. It was a common route into employment for a young girl. Margaret was a shy girl born out of wedlock though caringly brought up; she accepted the strict disciplines as a housemaid at Sutton Bingham and then East Coker, where, in the big houses, the staffs – inside and outside – were large, and the choice of a husband, opportunistic and mainly innocent rather than carnal, was surprisingly wide-ranging though nurtured in such a practical way.

Her first real romance was one that lasted a lifetime. Dad was an estate worker at East Coker. This kind of convenient liaison wasn't uncommon. For many of them, where else would they have found a partner?.

Their courtship was conventional and probably self-conscious. When Margaret had half-days off at the weekend, they strolled Stoney Lane together, picked bluebells in Spin Wood and watched the trains rattle by. Not too many stopped at Sutton Bingham's small station then. By 1962 it had gone for good and long-time signalman Stan Norman, known to all the local passengers who used to go on one-day trips, to Seaton and Lyme Regis, was out of a job. In time, as part of an incongruous transformation of the valley, it took on a vista of billowing canvas with small sailing boats and an embryonic marina as this fringe of East Coker suddenly went confusingly middle-class – in keeping with the emerging 264-acre reservoir.

Long before that, the housemaid and the estate worker had married and moved into Verandah Cottage, clad delicately in its mellow mauve of creeper-intimacy, back off the road with a narrow footbridge over the stream that in rainy weather gushed down from the steep hills above the church. That was to be their home for more than 60 years during which their post office account never noticeably expanded to any degree. Not once, as far as I remember, did they express any neuroses of financial plight. None of the cottage dwellers seemed to. Perhaps it never entered their heads, back in the thirties, that they might ever aspire to better days, better furniture, better suits of clothes. They were resigned to the restrictions of the way they lived; they seldom pondered improved escape routes and more money, however marginal, from the squire's steward on a Friday night. There may have been a gruff kind of humour about the limitations imposed by their socially marooned existence but not as much bitterness as they had every right to bemoan. In his years as an estate worker – during which he often trudged at the start of the day up to three miles beyond distant Coker Wood with his mate Jim Hughes, a heavy ladder on their shoulders and a crosscut saw to give them balance – his highest wage was 35 shillings a week.

"Bloody awful way to earn a living," they would chorus with their mates. "And I've forgotten me onion." But then they'd laugh about it, perhaps relieved that in those melancholy days when the nation was again getting back some strength in its muscles after the ghastlier aspects of the Depression, they at least had a job. If only the wordy pontificating economists, who wrote whole forests of pretentious theory, had known what it was really like. They never really have.

Yet oddly the villagers didn't know what it was like, either. The men stropped their cut-throats twice a week and looked respectable for church and even occasionally bell-ringing practice. Their wives didn't buy new dresses; they picked up something cheap at the jumble sales. And they all ate well from their gardens, the vegetables fresh and crunchy. That was why Jim and my dad liked their big, raw onion, sliced expertly with the pocket knife they always carried as they made a rough sandwich from their hunk of bread, for the welcome and energetically earned mid-day break, washed down with cold tea.

*Dad (right), a ringer for more than sixty years,
with his best man, Dick Andrews*

I started school and grew up in such an environment. Our life was unremarkably frugal. Dad carved the painfully small joint on Sunday, our one proper and substantial meal of the week, and Mother laid out the knives and forks in advance with some pride. She'd seen how they did it when there were big parties at the Court and she had been enlisted to help bring on the food. On reflection I don't suppose we had much of a life. But not once was I conscious of our domestic frustrations or a sense of deprivation.

Dad tried to earn a few extra coppers. As the church sexton he cut the churchyard grass three times a year. He scythed skilfully between the stooping tombstones. I came on behind with a big wooden rake which left my fingers blistered. As far as I know, my father was paid five shillings a quarter for duties which for part of the year meant trimming the wicks and filling the hanging lamps alongside the aisles. It never struck me that the parochial church council was particularly ungenerous to its loyal part-time staff. I left the sums to my father.

From necessity, my father was a practical man. He was pleased with the way he pruned and experimented with his fruit trees, scooping up still steaming dung from the road along which Farmer Giles' industrious, bony wife had guided the half dozen or so shorthorns home for milking. Good fresh dung, instinctively used, was for Dad an old, trusted part of the apple-grafting process. As an improviser, he made a tool shed and a rabbit hutch for me out of scraps of wood. During the war, he rather melodramatically dug deep in the clay and fashioned a narrow, damp air-raid shelter. A couple of times we put on thick coats over our pyjamas and climbed down the crudely made steps to a miniscule row of seats below. To me, it was a minor feat of adventure and engineering, though I suspected that as a lovingly protected family we were more in danger of pneumonia than any stick of high explosive deposited from a German bomber. "They'm not going to bomb us, Frank," a few neighbours used to say reassuringly.

How much do young sons analyse their fathers? As I have mentioned, we didn't talk too much as a family. "Pass the bread, son," was a veritable paternal monologue. That absence of conversation didn't trouble me. I just assumed that all village people ate in silence. Maybe bigger families had more to say. I was an only child; and on reflection, it was a familiar pattern in our parish. Years later I asked my parents about this. "Couldn't afford any more young 'uns, son." So in the early thirties, parsimony was a crucial part of the reason, certainly nothing to do with exploratory rural birth control.

Verandah Cottage had a surpringly large garden. The verandah as such had long gone. In its place were the pebbles leading up to the front door and the tenderly nurtured flowers around the small lawn. My father was inordinately proud of his garden: the size of his onions and parsnips, the way he brought on his Brussel sprouts, the mathematical precision of his rows, those early potatoes planted unfailingly on Good Friday and ready to eat ahead of the neighbours – or so it seemed to me. When relatives came to visit us on the occasional Sunday afternoon, a warm-hearted and yet solemn business, part of the accepted ritual was to go on a tour of the garden. Compliments were rightly paid to Frank. I was usually bringing up the rear of the horticultural procession

"This young lad of yours. Is he goin' to be a gardener, too?" There'd be a polite little laugh. "Hope so," I'd say, mostly to please my father.

Privately I thought it wasn't at all a bad job. I liked the smell of the soil; liked being entrusted to fork the first new potatoes of the season; liked hand-weeding the rows of burgeoning vegetables so that they suddenly looked neat and attractive. Yes, perhaps I'd be a gardener. The simple operation of planting the seeds and watching them emerge through the freshly raked soil appealed to me.

On weekdays, after school, I would walk along the road past cottages where old men, bent with arthritis, wizened from years of unrewarded labouring, looked into space. They may not have seemed particularly bright and intelligent. In truth, their own education had been grimly superficial. Their conversation was no more than a nod of recognition to the baker as he went past with his horse and two-wheeled bread van. The tin loaves were still warm and they were not long out of the Pulman ovens in Tellis Cross. No-one would ever have dared to call the old, weary men artists as they leaned on their gates. Yet they were. Their flower beds, which they were too modest to display in any ostentatious way, were beautiful, kaleidoscopic, arranged in designs that came, in the manner of a true painter, straight from their heads and imaginations. Nothing in East Coker in those apparently vacuous days was more life-enhancing than the flowers: the gentle manner they were planted, the unself-conscious love bestowed on them by bent, grimy fingers that never needed a brush and easel to portray such a spontaneous achievement of creativity.

The injustice was that they didn't even realise what floral beauty they had created. Their neighbours also trudged past a hundred times a day, offering no more than a token glance. "What's thee tiddies like this year, Bill?" Country dwellers didn't talk about their flowers; that was their secret indulgence.

In the years that followed those back-garden observations, I pondered increasingly the criminal wastage of talent. The old fellers from the village had so much to offer, but there was never really an outlet for their endeavours to be appreciated. It was unthinkable, of course, that there might be. So many, it appeared to me more and more, simply lived, laboured and died. There was no scope to tap their untutored, too often unnoticed talents and embrace their sheepish gifts. Only decades later do we accept the tragedy of such shameful wastage.

I come back to my father again. Almost all of his work was physical. The images I retain of him were of sharpening his scythe at the whetstone, of proudly surveying his deep trenches as the main-crop potatoes went in, holding his breath as he brought a wheelbarrow load of human excrement from the lavatory to the potential carrot patch. He had a well-muscled body and conversely – endearingly, too – fingers that were, although engrained, pale and delicate. We never discussed music, though I came to realise his frustration that he had no opportunity to learn an instrument. When I was six he went to a music shop in our home town of Yeovil and bought me a piano. It cost £35 and it must have considerably stretched the domestic resources.

I think he had visions of me becoming the church organist in time. "Up to you now, son. Mrs Hackwell has said she'll take you on." She was the organist and choir mistress. In fact, I made reasonable progress and passed the first two exams. Then I confessed to her that I hoped one day to join a dance band. Such a philistine intention took her by surprise. But, with the kindest of responses, she gave me a music book of supposedly tango dancing, for my next birthday. I saw it as a gesture of despair, however, that my involuntary fingers were not cut out one day to succeed Mrs Hackwell at the St Michael's church organ. I just didn't feel I could take syncopated liberties with Purcell – or even with relatively staid Latin-American melodies. The piano wasn't an unnecessary purchase. I painstakingly thumped out my depleted, shallow versions of *I'm forever blowing bubbles* and *Danny Boy* to let my father know I really did have a lingering affection for music, preferably if I could fantasise a little and imagine that I was on the stand with Geraldo or Roy Fox.

There were times when I could hear my father humming snatches from war-time songs like *Dolly Gray*. He also possessed a miniature clapped-out accordion which I believe he picked up for sixpence at Sherborne's Pack Monday fair. He would loop a piece of string around his thumb, where once there had been a leather strap, and I would hear him practising, clumsily and inexpertly, Christmas carols and pop songs of his day. I found it very moving and I crept away, not to be seen. I got the impression that he would have loved to be a proper musician. Was that another case of unfulfilled creative desire? In the same way, we didn't have many books in the house, apart from a small selection of detective fiction, with Mrs Henry Wood also well represented, that had been passed on at some time from Coker Court.

In the latter years of his life, he went back to his books. By then the number had been extended. He picked up books regularly from the mobile library that travelled round Coker's by-ways. The television became redundant for him, as his hearing deteriorated, and he spent hours reading and obviously enjoying the narratives. He retained an affection for detective stories, mixed in less gory fashion with an unlikely quota of sugary historical romance. He ranged unpredictably from Thomas Hardy to, yes, Barbara Cartland. But he was becoming an insatiable reader – and that delighted me.

When handsome Coker Court was sold, a victim of death duties, Dad needed to go for other work. For a time he ran – energetically though with a negligible profit – the Big House's walled gardens. He grew lovely peaches and nectarines, dug the whole big garden with a spade and put in too many hours. There was other employment as an insurance agent cycling round Yeovil's back streets and as a school caretaker in Yeovil and Sherborne. He liked working in a school environment. During the war years he had a spell looking after a market garden where he was a big favourite with the sixth formers. At one point he had more than half the grammar school's first XV in his greenhouse for a lunchtime smoke.

He was quite a charmer in his way. Pretty girls weren't ignored and he liked to pick a red or yellow rose from his garden and give it to them. I am not sure what Mum made of that flirty nature – but I doubt if she ever knew. As pensioners the pair of them had a more financially relaxed life. Dad liked to replenish his cider supply with the occasional visit to Sonny White's at Hardington, a locally famous repository for potent apple juice, or a Sunday morning call after ringing on farmer Billy Richards, where it was said the congregation in one of his barns was invariably more numerous than for matins at St Michael's. Frank and Margaret also both acquired a civilised taste for a glass of wine. Whisky remained a treat for my father. That opportunity of a heavy-handed dram would generate the inevitable piece of doggerel from him:

Whisky when you're well makes you sick
Whisky WILL make you well when you're sick

It's an ancient truism and it was much admired, and quoted. by my father.

He also liked to quote, with understandable pride, the inscription to George Foot on a headstone in Upcerne churchyard in Dorset, not far from where Jack Foot, my grandfather, was born. George's parents, William and Mercy, had died in the Cerne Abbas workhouse. Their son George had himself died in January 1923 after almost a lifetime working on the Upcerne estate. The headstone described him as 'faithful and devoted'. And there followed this rare and heartfelt verse:

For forty years he lived in Upcerne Wood
He saw the change of nature's varying mood
The Summer's sun, the winter starlight clear
The birds and flowers, the fleet and timid deer
These wonders by God to him were given
A Sacrament which pave the path to Heaven

Loyalty was apparently always a strong quality within the family, whatever its meagre sum total of worldly wealth.

My parents,
influential in their varying ways on what must have at times
seemed to them a confusingly versatile working life

3

DAMPIER AND DEFOE

As for many village boys at that time, the Church threatened to be a dominant factor in my life. Not, I confess with some guilt, that God and the theatrical rituals that surrounded him, had anything like as much influence on me as perhaps they should have. We used to sing in the choir because it brought us a grudgingly donated 3s 6d a quarter, with an extra sixpence or two if our mellifluous tones were incorporated in the vocal accompaniment for a local wedding. Beneath those stiff white collars and freshly ironed surplices lurked wayward notions.

As a choirboy in the churchyard

God may have nominally recruited us to be on his side, though in some ways he emerged badly from the arrangement. On balance, when it came to spirituality, he wasn't the clear winner. We may have projected an image of pure-eyed piety, as Mrs Hackwell, prim in her Sunday best, peered down proudly on us from her organist's mirror. But during those long, insufferably boring passages in the vicar's sermon, we were inclined to stray markedly from the Anglican rule-book.

With some ingenuity we perfected a succession of aerial dog fights (remember the war and the Spitfire era were not so far away) across the hallowed chancel where the other half dozen of the choirboys were ensconced in seeming attentiveness. Surreptitiously we checked our armaments and embattled fuselages as we dutifully awaited the call from the control tower to attack.

Our cassock pockets were already prepared for conflict. Hymn sheets were transformed into the best Fighter Command could offer. The planes had been expertly fashioned, in the way schoolboys used to: heavier in the nose to ensure momentum in initial flight. And when the torpid scriptures emanating from the pulpit reached their nadir, these pre-Battle of Britain boys went into action. The whole operation could be carried out with a surprising precision. If we controlled the trajectory, making sure it escaped the organist's limited range of vision, it was a pretty good method of passing the time during a dire address.

Little could have been more irreligious. Nor, of course, could have been the improvised larceny on choir-practice night in the summer months, once we'd escaped the tiresome rehearsal of all things Ancient and Modern. We'd run down the church path, climb over a fence and then help ourselves to the juicy pears, trained against the outside of the walled garden. Criminal? Surely not. The fruit belonged to Coker Court; the paternal Heneage family, regular church-goers and with their own box for themselves and their weekend guests, wouldn't have complained if someone had told them of such fruit-picking liberties. I'm not so sure about Tom Gilham, the stern-faced head gardener at the Court.

I spent hours, in the practical if not the spiritual sense, in or near the church. I liked its fusty smell, the sound of the carillon every three hours, the ancient pews, the peal of eight bells and the bicep sweat from the ringers on balmy evenings; all those tombstones, too, with lettering obscured by the weather over the generations, and yews nearly as old as the church itself. When I had wound the clock for my father and my work was done, I would climb onto one of the large tombstones and look down across the parish: seeing the way the smoke was drifting in unison in the gentle breeze from all the cottagers' wood fires. There was the village pub with its distinctive white facing and the cosy mellowness of the honeyed Ham stone along the main roads. I could see the washing on the line, the neat pattern of back gardens and, above all, I could sense the silence. There was nothing to hear but Mr Bath's faithful old bus.

As far as I remember, I never thought much about God. None of us boys did. There were other matters to stir our imagination. Would Portsmouth win the cup final? Who was this podgy bloke Mussolini, suddenly seeming to be getting far too covetous? Or, of more immediate concern, which of us were going to take part in the customary obstacle race around the lawns at North Coker House as part of the next Saturday's annual fete? One of the obstacles involved crawling under a large canvas sheet. Every year prompted the same question. Were stinging nettles deliberately placed across the grass under the canvas? Was there really someone on the organising committee with sadistic tendencies? In such varied flights to challenge our imagination, religion could frankly not expect too much of a youthful airing.

Schoolboys had enough in their heads without wondering why their parents went dutifully to evensong, and the more devout ringers came straight down from the belfry to join them. The men put on ties, awkwardly tied, for the weekly occasion of nominal worship. They knew the words of the familiar hymns, and it didn't seem to matter that they sang out of key and tune. Mum had a quite sweet if timid voice. Dad unfailingly took a packet of humbug sweets with him, to be retrieved from the pocket of his frayed suit and then noisily sucked during the sermon. As sexton he perhaps thought he had the necessary authority to be oblivious to any reaction from 'the old man'. Certainly in later life, as his hearing deteriorated, my father was even more unmindful of causing clerical offence. The sweets were still sucked with saliva-spattered relish before he passed the packet somewhat reluctantly along the pew. He yawned intermittently, an extended gesture with high-decibel sound effects as he slapped his mouth in climax to demonstrate an ageing countryman's weariness. My mother used to whisper with a hint of exasperation: "Do it quietly, Frank, for heaven's sake" (a quaintly appropriate choice of metaphorical location). "Make it look as though you're interested." It became a family joke. "It's his way of telling the parson that he's gone on long enough."

No, God didn't really have too much of a look-in when it came to intellectual affairs. Mrs Ray was probably totting up the week's meagre takings in her head. as she sat in her favourite pew. Tom Hackwell was wondering whether he had enough wood for the two unscheduled requests for coffins. Cockles Stevens, who sometimes read the lesson with the same booming, assertive voice he used as the local goalkeeper when calling for a back-pass, was no doubt reliving those prodigious goal kicks that effortlesssly threatened to land in the next field to frighten Farmer Denning's sheep.

To the choirboys, the services were all too solemn and joyless. At Easter, Whitsun and Christmas time, the ritual was enlivened with a procession around the naves during the last hymn. That meant I usually carried the cross, ahead of the self-conscious line-up of choristers. Without the organist's musical support from the other end of the church, we must have sounded embarrassingly weak. But after all, we were stretching our legs – and discovering who else was in the congregation.

It didn't demand too much skill carrying the cross, high and quite heavy though it was. Instead, the role called only for a measure of geographical knowledge and confidence. The route was predetermined, and I was after all well versed in its turns before the ultimate return to the choir stalls. But there were distractions. One Easter, when the congregation was suitably large, I was so busy winking at my proud parents – our eyes were always straying during these processions – that I so nearly took the wrong turning. It needed a rapid hiss of reprimand from Teddy Tucker, one of our long-serving tenors, to avert what could have been a calamitous mix-up, more reminiscent of a Paul Jones dance at the village hall With an adept, drastic change of direction, which would have been a credit to an AA patrolman of those days, I narrowly avoided taking the whole dignified choir into the Tudor Hall of the adjoining Coker Court. The hymn was completed, without any further incident, enlivened by a touch of typical, if misplaced, syncopation by one of the older boys who always appeared to think he was a Harry Roy vocalist.

Dance hall imagery was in fact never too far away. Coker's Saturday dance could after all be the social highlight of the week. Farm worker Stan White, a nice, ever-willing man of simple tastes, would stand at the door and collect the shillings and sixpences while keeping a custodial eye on one or two lads who had convivially broken their journey with a pint or two of local cider on their way to the hop.

I seldom had much pocket money to spare but would creep through a back door before climbing up into the small functional balcony where the Stan Russell Band, usually no more than a trio, blew the dust off their stack of age-weary sheet music while encouraging me to squat in such obviously willing discomfort on their discarded overcoats. Stan played the badly tuned piano with a thumping, infectious abandon. He had Ernie Bull on the drums, a role later adopted by Stan's wife, who with simplicity and a natural sense of timing, stuck to the brushes and was doubtless forbidden from trying anything more fancy or ostentatious. I loved secreting myself in the balcony of the village hall on those Saturday nights. It was a position of privilege, and I felt I was in the presence of one of those top dance bands I used to hear on the wireless. The Stan Russell Trio, at times augmented, were high on my list of heroes. When it came to the quickstep, Stan's well-fleshed fingers would become mesmerically animated while his shiny shoes, always freshly polished I noticed, banged manically up and down on woodwork which at times I feared might splinter. Seventy years later I was still thumping in time with the music – and I put that rhythmic instinct down to Stan and his musical improvisers. On occasions I am sure they hit the wrong notes and forgot which key they were playing in. But no-one was aware of their flaws. In my idolatry I certainly wasn't.

They needed to thump to create the surging beat because they had nothing as sophisticated as a microphone. There was a marvellous brute force about this depleted orchestra and the strident sequence of pop favourites they paraded with such gusto.

The dancers never complained, although I suspect it was the band that lost its way in some of the more rigid three-four time and the relatively complicated slow foxtrot numbers. I liked to peep over the balcony rails to watch the dancing. The steps varied markedly in execution and basic skill. But it was all polite and proper. Locals may have privately resented seeing their pretty partners whisked away during the 'Excuse me' dance. They didn't show it, however. As far as I remember – even if such nuances meant little to me then – there was nothing overtly suggestive or sensual on the dance floor. Husbands and wives held each other around the waist or the shoulders. They concentrated on the steps and said little to each other until the band finished its clutch of three numbers. Then there would be the obligatory wholesome applause and timid, mutual thank-yous as they returned to their seats.

Couples, not just the married ones, were inclined to be self-conscious as in their often awkward way they moved round the floor. It was all surprisingly well behaved. They had seen in the magazines how the expensively gowned, American film stars and their black-tie escorts did it. This was the nearest East Coker – dreaming with a touching unreality and simplicity of inaccessible heights of social grandeur – got to that. At least they all privately pretended. On Monday morning the young men of the parish would be back at the twine works, the saw mills or harnessing the cart horses in anticipation of another day's unglamorous labour. The girls would neatly fold the plain dresses they had made themselves, maybe reflecting on a flattering compliment they had earned during the last waltz as male loins eventually burned in unfulfilled arousal. Rural working-class existence didn't offer too much. And indeed not too much was expected.

As we moved into the late 1930s, I listened more intently to the news on the wireless or studied with greater awareness the headlines on my grandfather's *News Chronicle*. Who was this Adolf Hitler, I often asked myself? I began to hear the word 'appeasement', however, and was goaded to look it up. And I sensed that this Hitler wouldn't escape from our nation's consciousness. Gradually he made me feel uneasy. I've no idea how many boys suffered similar confusion. Boys and girls still struggling with their nine-times table don't as a rule go in for an analysis of power politics. I wasn't by some distance the brightest lad in our class, but I think I started to worry more than most of the others. I had been told, however sketchily, conflictingly and maybe melodramatically, something of the horrors of trench warfare in the 1914-18 conflict. It was not easy to imagine this alongside the peace and hollyhocks of my home, Verandah Cottage.

Village people may have restricted vocabularies, often finding it hard to articulate their uneasiness. Sid (Tammy) Neville, who lived at Ten Houses, on the edge of the parish, was one with strong opinions he was never inhibited about expressing. He worked at the twine factory and cycled past my garden path twice a day. His voice was loud and likeable, his views unequivocal. Sid, who bowled unpretentious seamers for the local team, let us all know if he had something to share. I was standing at the gate one day and Sid was in apparent intellectual earnestness as he cycled home at mid-day, as assertive as he was hungry.

Looking in my direction but intending to address anyone within listening distance, he hollered: "This Hitler, he's an evil and greedy bastard. Wants to be friendly with us but I don't trust him."

I was transfixed. I had never heard him swear before and didn't realise that he had even a passing interest in the way Germany was surreptitiously sharpening its swords. European geography or even a whisper of Teutonic history were certainly not on my school curriculum. Sid's chilling words never left me. About the same time, actually at one of Stan Russell's dances, I eavesdropped from my balcony vantage point on an agitated conversation wafting up from the hall between quicksteps. "We'm all goin' into the army before long. And I reckon it'll be just as bad as the last bloody time, Arthur."

More swearing, more impassioned opinion. As an unknowing lad, I trembled.

Earlier I revealed the extent to which I was magnetically drawn to St Michael's church, the building itself, its smells and history if not the challenges of faith. I liked to wander into the church when it was empty. I would stroll the side aisles and peer up at the stained glass windows or fading inscriptions of local dignitaries with elongated names.

There was also work to be done as the sexton's son. I refilled the paraffin can before it was taken by my father, perching always a little precariously up a wooden ladder as he attended the hanging lamps. Outside, I shovelled the coke into manageable piles, to be heaved into the roaring old-fashioned furnace, intended, if inadequately, to heat the church in winter. At times I cunningly played truant when sent off to wind the clock, taking the heavy iron key – on reflection keys seem to have been a crucial part of my life and ecclesiastical adventures – to unlock the base of the tower. Then I would climb, enraptured as ever, up the uneven steps of the spiral staircase, past the belfry and the clock room, all the way to the confined, evocative summit. For half an hour I'd stand up there at the top of the tower, gazing down in awe at the parish of my birth.

Below me at one side was Coker Court – with its lawn and circular fishpond, its Georgian wing and a hundred different shades and fragrances of lilacs. This was the Colonel's floral passion. He did the pruning himself. At daffodil time, too – there was what seemed to me an unmatched profusion along the sylvan walks where the family happily wandered before their evening aperitif. Tom, the head gardener, would in canny rotation select two boys from the village school to snap off the decaying heads and cart them to an obscure tip. We were not generously paid for our duties but were given a free lunch as a boost to our minimal wages. The school had briefed us to be on our best behaviour. Our lunch, or dinner as we always called it in those days, was taken in the servants' quarters. We knew our place – and our time limit. Mr Gilham, with the erect posture and stern demeanour of a martinet policeman rather than a pastoral planter of seeds and follower of country lore, would allow us 45 minutes. Then he'd interrupt Joan Boucher the cook's succulent home-made apple tart and tell us which daffodil walks still needed to be attended. We could probably have benefited from a timely, latter-day word or two from an intrepid union official, spelling out our fledgling rights. So, of course, in those years of haphazard labour organisation would every man who worked the land. For him it was long unrelenting hours and a back bent from the uncompromising demands of the hay or harvest field. And no apple tart from comely Mrs Boucher.

Now here I was, looking down from the top of the tower, learning to think gradually, hesitatingly for myself – wondering, for the first time, just why life had been so unfair for some, so privileged or lucky for others. How would it pan out for me?

Dad would not have approved of my solitary enterprise, the adventures of my tender years, as I climbed to one of East Coker's highest points. In truth I was no stranger to the cobwebs, the redundant jackdaw nests in the crumbling window slits and the tingling spooky feel of the spiral staircase which led to my private realm of high-altitude power and perspective. Spooky it truly was as darkness approached – and that was part of the appeal.

It took me nearly a quarter of an hour to wind the chimes. The primitive contraption creaked as I crouched and wound the thick rope, sometimes inventing my own dastardly, imaginative tales as I did so. All the time the big clock ticked inexorably on. Approaching twilight produced its own range and shapes of shadows. The ghostly mood should have filled me with fear but I knew I had been expected to visit the clock-room earlier when it was lighter and that I ought not to have spent so much time at the top of the tower. But that was when it was most compelling.

Years later I could still see those scurrying shadows and hear that metallic tick-tock. I would never lose anything as vivid as that. It was creepy and macabre. And it gave me my first published short story, rather melodramatically called 'The Tower and the Tombstone'. I lacked literary confidence and wrote, with some native loyalty, under the name of David Coker. It was accepted by an evening paper whose resident artist and cartoonist supplemented my story with a suitably fearsome illustration. I was thrilled, even if a little less lifted by the size of the one-guinea cheque.

Empty churches are singularly eerie as dusk approaches. The pews take on their nightly smell. Mice emerge to chase each other in search of harvest festival remnants. Rooks peck away in the rafters. The Bible on the lectern is closed as if it is no longer time for prayer ....

I was transfixed, never frightened as far as I recall, by the darkening ambience. I could still make out the names on the war memorial. Then I'd move a few yards along the south aisle to the brass tablet on the wall, commemorating the seafaring and navigational feats of the village's greatest sailor, William Dampier. He and his conflicting achievements were for me a viewing obsession. I would squint at the brooding facial features and then regularly read, sometimes aloud, the words I could barely understand and certainly not pronounce. He was a navigator – the best of his day – explorer and buccaneer. But how was I supposed to know what a hydrographer was, or what it meant that he had circumnavigated the globe three times? Long words troubled and irritated me. They still do.

Over my youthful, unworldly years, Dampier remained a distant idol. On my way home from school I would often pause to look at the handsome thatched building, once a farm, where he was born in 1651. Hymerford House stood back from the main road and a stream snaked round its back garden. It had a decorative porchway as well as an air of mystery. The occupants, when I lived in the village, kept to themselves. I must admit I didn't really know too much about Dampier – in truth, few did – but I was aware that he had his place in our maritime history. One day in an amiable break-time argument at school I rashly claimed that he was more important than Nelson. I rightly lost that one, though I suppose I had done my best to laud the virtues of a local man.

William Dampier

In the decades that followed I often contemplated and quietly questioned some of Dampier's qualities; it was perhaps an act of partial geographical disloyalty on my part. Hero worship, whether it involves the cruel sea or a cricket match, is fraught with broken human sign-posts and misjudgements. He charted, for instance, the Australian coastline and much more as his vessels stumbled on uninhabited islands. He was a brilliant, self-educated scientist who observed and chronicled bird and plant life as well as the caprices of the waves. His aids to navigation were sparse and often primitive. He recorded his discoveries in dozens of storm-stained notebooks and on scraps of paper, much of which was later published to acclaim.

Dampier once met the Queen, and not many young men from my village did that. Yet he was never quite as recognised as he deserved to be. Nor were the personal rewards substantial. Some of his privateer commissions flopped, leaving his backers to scowl and roundly blame him. He fell short on leadership skills, too frequently rowing with his crews and some senior officers. He was notoriously petulant and fiery. And he was fined after one court martial appearance.

For a long time I used to pause alongside his brass tablet, proud of his achievements and what I saw as a boundless sense of courage and swashbuckling adventure. He died in 1715, and I could never quite understand why his life had tailed away into relative anonymity, leading to an unknown grave. But I was glad that East Coker had not forgotten him. There were 250th and 300th anniversary church services to mark and celebrate his life. The local schoolchildren were encouraged to take part in fancy dress parades. Civic dignitaries put on their chains of office to honour Dampier's memory.

Flushed by selective, colourful tales, and not yet aware of TS Eliot's metaphysical forays into poetry, I nominated Dampier for years as my parish's most illustrious resident. I would quote with affected knowledge how as a boy he'd hitched lifts to the Dorset coast, just to sniff the salty air, before being apprenticed to a ship's master at Weymouth. So much for the Latin books he had rejected. It all made sense to me. East Coker may have been no more then 20 miles from the sea but it belonged in spirit to maritime adventure. Why else did the village still have a sail-cloth tradition? Romance was apt to blur my level of accuracy. I fear that at times it still does. I can think of greater flaws.

I return to my qualifications about hero-worship. There was plenty of time, as I prowled the church's south aisle, to study the explorer's facial features. His nautical contemporaries all remarked about his brooding, unsmiling appearance. The eyes were dark and hard. Sadly they belonged to the plunderer as much as to the observer of natural history. And this brings me to the undeniable paradoxes of the man whose savagery and occasional sadism, at least partly excused by the insubordination and mutiny among his crews, increasingly fascinated me and changed my view of him. The disparate crewmen drank and argued too much. Some had been recruited with difficulty and few assurances in the rough-and-ready alcoholic haze of a Bristol quayside – and it showed. He meted out brutal punishment to the offenders. Alternative attitudes from fellow officers and meddling amateur navigators weren't encouraged. There were varying opinions about his bravery in battle. He had an astute glint in the eye when it came to distributing the invariably modest pirates' spoils. It doesn't look as though he was the most endearing of companions on one of those long, taut voyages. He was happier, I like to think, studying his improvised maps, leaving the argumentative sailors to sort out their constant quarrels.

Maybe it was the influence of St Michael's church, where he was baptised, that gave him traces of a strong moral code, while adding to the contradictions in his character. He didn't hold with the strong drinking. Women, smuggled on board ship, were far too much of a distraction. One negress, taken on as a cook though altogether too wanton with her bodily favours, was publicly flogged on Dampier's orders.

In those wide-eyed schoolboy days of mine I interpreted just what I wanted from that tablet's brass lettering. I never attempted to read *New Voyage Round the World*, the compendium of extraordinary knowledge he somehow found time to acquire and set down in print. Neither, for some reason or other, did I ever read *Robinson Crusoe*. I left my friends to tell me what happened. But the link with Defoe, no stranger to the taverns of the West Country where he expertly eavesdropped, is real enough. He heard, at first hand, the way that on Dampier's last voyage, the obstinate Alexander Selkirk was rescued after being marooned alone for more than four years on the island of Juan Fernandez.

Defoe, the most vigilant of listeners and skilful of writers, seized on the priceless human episode to incorporate into *Robinson Crusoe*. I insist that Dampier deserves much more of the literary credit than came his way from this timeless 'survival' classic for young readers.

4

FEUDAL DAYS

Colonel and Mrs Walker-Heneage in effect ran the village. They were Lord and Lady of the Manor, visually respected for their position in West Country society and their envied reputation as landowners. They also had a somewhat awesome, inaccessible presence, part of the rigidly structured pattern then of rural life. Once they owned, it seemed, almost every property in the parish. The powerful link went back to the middle of the 16th century.

East Coker was a definitive feudal village, picture-book in appearance, disproportionate in wealth and possessions. The divisions were pronounced, though those who lived within its attractively delicate and locally quarried boundaries simply accepted the unfairness of the way things were. They did their moaning at home, out of authoritarian earshot. Some of my boyhood elders thought they could detect the start of subtle changes, shafts of overdue radical light. I'd grown up in a homely, thick-walled country cottage well before such luxuries as electricity and lavatories with a chain had been introduced. It never occurred to me that, if I were patient enough, modest benefits might one day be on the way.

Verandah Cottage, wrapped in those varying shades of Virginia creeper, vibrant with the first spring indications of burgeoning vegetation and the sweet perfume of its flowers, was a particular favourite of the Heneages. It's true that they never progressed beyond the front door step, to notice the depleted basic furniture. But they would inquisitively peer through the living room window, perhaps to admire the sturdy oak beams and speculate how long they had been there.

We needed to keep our heads down for safety as in rotation we sat in the solitary armchair near the winter logs. Mother avoided danger as she did the cooking on the open fire. Within the family she was known as 'asbestos fingers'. She never seemed to get burnt as she constantly threw escaping red-hot wood back on the blaze with her naked hands. "Blow me – that were HOT warm," she'd exclaim, emphasising the capital letters in one of her quaint hard-to-explain West Country expressions. The room was always dark, I recall, and it was time to light the oil lamp in the winter weeks by early afternoon.

Outside, Dad had staked the wire netting for us to have a few hens and newly laid eggs. At Christmas time he grabbed the fattest, squawking Rhode Island, tied its legs together and hung it in wretched submission from a big nail driven into the wall. He then stunned the hen before slitting its throat. The whole process was done swiftly, efficiently and without a hint of sentimentality. I used to watch, not squeamishly but trying to disguise any outward sign of unease.

"Nice one, son, for Christmas dinner. Go nice it will with some of yer mother's stuffin'. Just leave it there to bleed for a bit." I was never quite sure how long the death throes took. It did usually appear, though, that there were still despairing flutters of feathers a minute or two after my father's versatile pocket knife had been wiped off and put back into a grimy trouser pocket. Working-class boys, even those like me with a sensitive nature, weren't expected to wince. Dad was a creature of countryside culture. He liked the idea of a fleshy Rhode Island for Christmas. Not that he was fastidious. He cleared his plate, whether it was a bit of blackbird-and-rook pie or the rather more cherished slices of well-cooked poultry.

"Got a good breast on her, Dad." He would nod. Like his sister, Doll, my father served a busy, unpaid apprenticeship at one of the lodges where his own father was the gamekeeper, cornering rabbits and then pulling their necks. If he'd ever recoiled, it would have been detected as a sign of weakness. In any case the rabbits, dozens of them, were killed for the stew-pot. Mother skinned them with perfunctory skill. There were so many running wild that they were caught with ease as they chased blindly into the netting, held strategically by Frank and his sister.

Colonel Heneage knew nothing, of course, about such practical preparations for the table. His peak-capped chauffeur would drive him down from the Court at times on a Sunday between services, to check on the cosmetic appearance of his trees in the paddock, just along the road from my home. "The Old Man's around," I'd hear Dad say to Mother. He had this instinct to sniff out the Colonel's approach, especially during the week when there were decaying branches to be cut in Spin or Coker Wood and the two woodmen were resting to share a Woodbine.

It often struck me that when he was driven down to the village, getting out of his big car to stroll along the main road, the villagers would withdraw into their back rooms. He was a kindly man but he intimidated them. For their part, they didn't know how to address him. He had a patrician voice which he would direct in commanding tones at Tom Gilham or the estate steward, Mr Wild. You came when you were called – even from the relative obscurity of the back room. His military background wasn't lost on you. Colonel Heneage served in the Grenadier Guards, mentioned in despatches five times during the 1914-18 war. His wife, Dorothy, was the last of the influential Helyar line. Their only son, David, who died in 1950, had followed his father into the Grenadier Guards. He left the army for a time, becoming managing director of Fortnum & Mason, before rejoining the Guards as a major to serve throughout the 1939-45 war. The Heneage and Helyar dynasties were proud of their estate and bulging workforce.

At Mrs Heneage's funeral service the moss-lined coffin was borne by six of the long-serving estate workers, one of them my father. The butlers, footmen, cooks, house and scullery maids … they monopolised some of the longer pews. The tears, for the Colonel, and then his widow, were genuine enough.

The Lord of the Manor and his Lady may have been metaphors of a fading, outdated culture. They represented privilege and the rich pickings from the land and recovering stocks and shares. But from their lofty social perch, far removed by circumstances from physical labour as well as distanced psychologically from the workers' negligible back-pocket existence of coppers gratefully grasped on Friday pay nights, there was an odd kind of affection, mutually returned. Only in more recent times was I fully aware of it.

East Coker Boys' Club
with Mrs Heneage, our patron, and Ivor Sanders, the vicar

When I went down with scarlet fever as a ten-year-old, unable for a year to take my scholarship in search of a grammar school place, the Colonel and his wife regularly enquired about my health and even sent down a jar of calf's foot jelly "to speed your son's recovery". They gave little gifts like that to the needy, as well as sympathetic notes to the distressed and bereaved.

Yet feudal Britain, not just East Coker, knew and, in the case of the 'thinking poor' among them, grudgingly accepted its predestined place. There was really no scope to step outside its intractable bounds. One day, they vaguely imagined, they might be a little more like the Heneages and have that posh lav with a flush. Yes, one distant day. Looking back, I don't feel that my village went in too much for self-pity.

The parish chugged along, looking as pretty as ever, praised in print by Priestley, still not quite sure who the emergent TS Eliot was. Did this scholarly fellow really have nothing better to do than write a poem about the place where we lived? Particularly as we couldn't understand what he was on about.

The routine of community life was sorted out, as well as it could be. The men grew their own vegetables. Pulman's bread was brought, crusty and still warm, by pony cart. Reg Griffin could find time for a chat with most housewives. He wore his cap at a memorably jaunty angle, obscuring one eye completely. But the horse knew the route. The butcher called once a week and so, if we were lucky and there was enough loose change in the egg cup on the dresser to meet our humble needs, did the fish man. I would also watch, in admiration of such muscular prowess, the coalman, balancing a hundredweight of jagged South Walean lumps in a sack on his bruised shoulders, after the coal had been heaved off the lorry to be awkwardly carried up our long front path to the improvised coal shed. And there was the ironmonger, who brought us the heavy accumulator for the wireless.

Sidney Thorne looked after the village stores, a conscientious man who took on a sort of Pickwickian appearance after a good day and picked up the remnants of trade after the delivery people from Yeovil had come and gone. His range of goods, however, didn't progress as far as those of one of his successors, Bob Moger, who wasn't afraid to experiment in the early radical stages of rural culinary skills. He once had a good run on rook pie. "Shot by meself," his chalked board outside the shop boldly claimed. We didn't see so much of Mrs Thorne, and the rumour dispensers, apt to gather outside the stores, used to say that "she liked a drop."

From my self-imposed position, at the side of the cottage behind the Worcester Pearmain apple tree, I liked to see the tradesmen call or at least pass by with loud blares on the horn or overworked rings of their cycle bells. The Walls ice-cream man came on a tricycle and was a popular visitor to the village once a fortnight, despite dirty finger nails and a fag unhygienically balancing between his well-thumbed packet of cigarettes and the ice cream he fashioned between two wafers as if laying concrete.

Not all callers were predictable. An elderly chap came offering to sharpen our scissors or shears. He had gentle fingers like Dad as he ran his moistened whetstone along his scythe before cutting the graveside grass, and I was now transfixed by the practised manner the scissors-man perched on his specially transformed bike to give our knives and garden sickles a murderous edge.

And who else did I watch with admiration from my hidden all-eyes position? The chimney sweep, with so many brushes it was a miracle he stayed on his cycle, turned his visits into occasions. We'd string up an old sheet to keep the dust away as he disappeared halfway up the chimney. I always worried that he might not come down again. I much liked him, enough to make one of my infrequent appearances of close-up curiosity. "Go and make Jack a nice cup of tea, David." I did what I was told, mystified that he had sufficient sight through the caked, sweaty soot to know where to put the spoon.

It was the gypsies who terrified me as an unworldly schoolboy. From time to time they pulled in their caravans at Pincushion Corner; from there, the women started knocking at doors to sell their clothes pegs. "Hello, laddie, where's missus then?" I was usually tempted to lie and say she wasn't at home, so that I could escape from this intimidating figure with the cruel leathery face and a voice of nomadic patois I could only sketchily understand.

But Mother would make her untimely entry and make it clear we needed no clothes pegs. I remember several times when a gypsy caller eventually worked out that there was no call for pegs or bunches of lavender. "Then I'll put a curse on thee." She said it with menace, making me shiver. She would look back as she stormed down the front path. "And don't 'ee forget it. A bleedin' curse on thee and thee family."

Not everyone who called hoping to make a sale frightened me, of course. Fred, from down at Ten Houses, was a useful feller to have around the place. That was if you had a domestic animal out of sorts. I don't know about Fred's qualifications as a homespun vet but most of his solutions seemed to work. He also specialised in castrations – with the aid of a steady hand and a bottle of disinfectant They used to say the village would have been overrun with cats but for Fred's busy schedule in neutering surgery.

East Coker was a poor though happy village. Just as there was ready humour about Fred's spaying techniques, so there was about the love life of Johnny Hibbs. He was the local rag-and-bone man, though in fact he collected in his pony cart almost anything that was going spare. His piercing voice rang out along the cottages. "Got anything for us, missus?" Johnny's voice was loyally, lovingly in the plural. His long-time partner was Carrie. They were an ageing impassioned couple, who drove their weary pony of protruding bones on a daily, mostly unremunerated, journey around the south Somerset and Dorset lanes. Their love for each other was touchingly steadfast. Most nights, they would share a glass of ale and then sleep, just off the side of the road at Coker Marsh, in the open air. If it rained, they sheltered under one of the trees. Most people liked Johnny and Carrie. And they must have wondered how the devoted couple ever made a living.

Perhaps I will be allowed, within the lighter side of country life and its oddball freelance tradesmen, to mention an endearing maverick relative of mine, always known in the family as Uncle Harry. He worked for farmers, thatchers, estate agents and gamekeepers. For speed and proficiency, no-one could touch him. He was famed for his hurdle and spar making. Everyone apparently wanted to employ him, particularly the numerous thatchers who marvelled at the rate of his hazel spar-making, which didn't drop much below 500 a day. But he was frugal in his spending and was content to walk miles in Hardy country to carry out a job, rather than catch a train and bus.

He was a genuine character, known by all the farmers who wanted some hurdles made well and at exceptional speed. Yet those same farmers also used to say with an ungenerous snigger that Uncle Harry was just a bit simple. They put it down with glib chuckles to the generally accepted rumour that he never quite recovered from a childhood accident, falling out of a tree, landing on his head, when collecting magpie eggs. Some of his actions gave strength to the tongue-in-cheek reports. He spoke slowly and would answer, out of sequence, questions put to him ten minutes before. His domestic life was apparently pretty sterile and amusingly irrational. He possessed a decent pocket-watch, wore it unfailingly and yet never wound it up. "Thas the way it'll wear out," he answered those who questioned why he never quite knew the time. "And me watch won't ever go wrong, how I do look after it." It wasn't certain whether he undressed when he went to bed. But not once did he take his bowler hat off before he lay down for the night. He certainly rejected the idea of underpants. Instead he'd buy cotton linings which he painstakingly sewed onto his trousers. My son, Mark, addicted to family folklore and especially Harry's eccentric lifestyle, discovered that this unrivalled spar-maker would remove his reinforced trousers every weekend, wash them, dry them in front of the fire and put them back on.

The stories about him are endless and, I am assured, mainly authentic. He once stayed with my parents when working for the Colonel, surprising my mother one evening by saying: "Misses, they bain't goin' to put any matches in my bed, are they? 'Twould catch me on fire." Like many of his whims and inconsequential statements, this one lacked point if not wayward charm.

My son's research revealed that Harry carried all his money around with him, stuffed in his various pockets. "Don't trust them damn banks, missus." Nor, as a rough-and-ready countryman did he trust the bulls. If he took a rest in a field of cattle, he made sure his back was against a sturdy tree trunk and that his eyes were on the alert. Bulls remained an obsession.

Harry cut his own hair. He had mirrors strategically positioned all round the room where he was then living. That gave him the chance to view his tonsorial adjustments from every angle. In the 1920s, in what appeared to be a typically impulsive move, he sailed for New Zealand to work for his brother Frank. It showed an unlikely streak of ambition. But he kept the ten-shilling notes in his pockets and returned to the familiar hazel spars and hurdles of Dorset and Somerset.

In one touching summary of his humble hopes, he said: "Gi' I a cottage, a garden and an orchard to grow some apples." Uncle Harry didn't aim high. His simple ambitions went unfulfilled. But he left instead a wealth of Wessex canniness and timeless eccentricity.

Up to the outbreak of the 1939 war, there was still work to be had locally. The men who didn't labour on the village farms, cycled to the Drake's webbing factory, where the order books weren't yet in decline and the reverberating hooter summoned reassuringly for the mid-day break or end of the day's work. The sawmills always carried a thick carpet of sawdust and the bracing odour of freshly cut timber.

And there was work for the young and older women. Yeovil prospered then as a centre of glove manufacture, with more than forty factories. Women were encouraged to do gloving at home. The work was brought to them. They weren't paid especially well but their earnings provided a useful supplement to their husbands' pittances.

Those were the years when I was most romantically captivated by all that East Coker offered. Mr Pomeroy, in his forge next to the village stores and opposite the school, was busy and, to me, fearless as he rested the heavy horses' legs between his thighs. He would wipe his nose against his soiled leather apron as, preoccupied, he went about his work. I ceaselessly feared he would be kicked as the horseshoe was moulded into a new pair of all-weather shoes. But as far as I knew, he never was. Back on the road, there was a reawakened sprightly arrogance about the newly shod horse. It carried a different step and sound. Or was I only imagining that? I spent hours gazing at Mr Pomeroy at work. The forge reeked of burning charcoal and, in the height of summer, human sweat.

This was when I saw East Coker at its best: the passing carter tugging on the reins, the thatchers shinning up the ladders with their bales of golden roofing. "And go careful with them fires, missus. Don't want any more like we had at Bradford Abbas last year."

It was a wise word of caution from one of the thatchers. You couldn't be too careful about chucking paper into the flame. At neighbouring Bradford Abbas a row of thatched cottages had been virtually destroyed. One of them was lived in by my Aunt Minnie. She lost many of her most treasured possessions; the rest were frantically piled onto the lawn, beyond repair. At Verandah Cottage, my parents' anxiety about loose shreds of paper catching the thatch was understandable. Dangerous blazes and precarious rescues from bedroom windows remained a serious risk in those years, when the ill-equipped firemen, agelessly brave and with meagre protective clothing, sometimes took a long time to augment their basic crews before locating some of those isolated farmhouses.

Despite such dramas and the daily shortcomings, we got on well as a community. Life could be lonely for those whose homes were on the outskirts of the village. Half-obscured farms relied on the company of the animals or a glass of the cider they had made themselves. On the edge of Coker Wood lived the Cox family, shy and remote. There were three brothers who unfailingly carried out a strange ritual each Sunday. After their six-mile cycle ride, they'd prop their bikes against the railings of the Quicksilver Mail inn at the top of Hendford Hill, still marginally within the Coker boundary. They never appeared to deviate from the location or destination of their ride. There they would remain for several hours, all eyes of innocent bewilderment as the traffic went by. As far as I could see, they hardly exchanged a word. Amid the spectacle of motorised excitement, they didn't feel they needed to.

They were a pleasant if embarrassingly quiet family. I can only assume that the Quicksilver Mail turning, with one road leading to Dorchester and another to Crewkerne, was to them like a visit to London or the unknown. They'd come to see the cars go by. I do hope it doesn't sound patronising that I found their repetitive and innocent weekly exercise – so different from their lives as farm workers during the week – moving in its sheer simplicity.

Not that the parish lacked entertainment, even if much of it was self-generated. The beech tree, centrally positioned and just over the road from the old village hall on one side and the school on the other, was a landmark of undisputed importance. It was where the bus stopped, where pubescent lovers held hands and older ones lived dangerously in the dark as they sheltered from the rain. It was where the whist drive timetable was announced on the wall poster – as was the football team for the following Saturday. "Team to meet at the Tree at 1.30 p.m. for the next away game" was the monolithic instruction. Some of us reckoned that the tree had local status to rival that of the church. When it eventually got blown down by an unnaturally ferocious wind in 1960, parishioners saw it in poignant, human terms and mourned its passing.

That was how I incorrigibly viewed a number of the trees in the village. I realised they were so much older, wiser and better proportioned than I ever was. When I did my National Service and was away for two years, I think I suffered from homesickness. I missed my parents, grandparents, my mates with whom I had liked to kick a ball or risk foolhardy singles in the closing overs, and the beech tree. There was an element of disloyalty in my romance. The tall, slender poplar at the edge of the paddock became my partner in a secret love affair. I used to be able to see her from my bedroom window, swaying sensuously in the gentle early-morning wind.

I have never seen a more supple or sexier tree. She knew how much she was admired. As a car or two spluttered by, she couldn't resist the temptation to show off, moving her dainty, naked hips with all the innate grace of a South Sea island dancer. She was beautiful and wicked at the same time. One night on RAF guard duty, desperately lonely and thinking perhaps with a slightly unnatural ardour of my wonderfully flirty poplar, I wrote an article all about her for the provincial weekly paper I had temporarily left behind. It was used, every cringing and fawning adjective of devotion, in the following Friday's issue.

I can't find too many good things to say about my days as a National Serviceman. But seeing my unashamed personal tribute to this wondrous mistress printed, for all the world to discover, self-indulgent as it was, took its place with my most joyful, elusive moments as a gauche sprog aircraftsman second class.

There was a semblance of injustice that my poplar never received the same acclaim and publicity as the beech. She didn't find herself emblazoned as a well-known meeting point on the village posters. Nor did she invite the locals to alight from their buses alongside her roots. But she caused men to catch their breaths. Walkers used to stop and peer up at her slimly tapered summit and I fancy she winked at them. It was enough to make me jealous.

In the summer months, one poster told us the date of the Women's Institute flower show, a highly competitive annual event in which masculine forearm muscles were flexed amid the horticultural rivalry. Another poster indicated that a garden fete would be held at Coker Court. That was a rarity, usually reserved for coronations and royal celebrations. The village school would be there in large numbers, to lead the maypole dancing and to hope that not too many this year got their ribbons in an embarrassing tangle.

These social events at the Court were handsomely enacted on the circular lawn at the top of the cedar drive. They carried a pleasing veneer of democracy. Mrs Heneage, gracious and deliberate, would wander from stall to stall, with fleeting words to schoolchildren quite overawed by her presence. They'd give a little self-conscious bow or curtsy if she was coming in their direction. The men, many of whom worked on the estate, liked to put on their best suits and a new flat cap which they touched deferentially as the Colonel spoke to them. It would be a surprise if he recognised many of them on one of those days when their coats and trousers were matching.

"Ay, yes, Dick isn't it. Are you going to win the pig?"

Nothing too feudal about that, surely. Christian names, something in truth he didn't discourage – from him, not them – and, after that, an almost chummy conversation about skittling for a pig.

The Colonel was invariably in a perfectly cut tweed suit and his regimental tie. His two golden retrievers, Lion and Tiger, remained at his side. He would point at them. "They like the music, you know."

One year, emboldened by the employer's willingness to pursue an infrequent chat with his worker, the Colonel was asked if he could hear the music coming from the Tudor almshouses just down the drive. He was told it was 'Daisy' Langdon, one of the male residents, having a practice on his fiddle. Daisy used to spend hours playing on his antiquated violin, although there was little evidence of the instrument ever being checked for tone or purity of note. Handel's *Largo* was one of his favourites. He'd often try to keep in tune with music drifting down from the Court. I'm not sure how successful his symphonic aspirations were when he did his best to keep up with the musical maypole dancers from the top of the drive.

The Colonel had two grandsons, Simon and Timothy. During their school holiday I was encouraged to play cricket with them on the lawn. It was a happy, relatively unselfconscious time. They disputed catches and run-outs like all boys of their age. I fancy they left me to do much of the chasing among the outfield of daisies. Our voices were different but not our enjoyment for the game. Simon, tall and upright, played his strokes correctly, just as he'd been taught in the school nets. Tim's approach was more jokey and frivolous. I was invited to join the tea-time session, I imagine, because of my parents' employment.

I was inclined to be podgy, not fast between the wickets. There was always a note of undisguised triumph as Simon walked back to his scruffed-out mark, having rearranged my stumps with a fastish, more than half-decent delivery. We played with kit newly purchased. There were only three of us but the Heneage boys liked to take their time strapping on their pads and making a slightly flamboyant arrival at the crease. Tim, the smaller of the two, always wore pads that were too big for him. We laughed together when he stumbled in search of a run.

Here, too, was embryonic democracy at work. I was inclined to be the silent member of the trio, accepting my suspect dismissals and joining the ritual applause when Simon carted the ball over the yew hedge and into the cow pats. I think the boys liked me. They didn't patronise or, as far as I know, mock me and my timorous ways. Only once did I get above myself. It was the early years of the war. We were at the front door of Coker Court, en route to the lawn, where one of the workmen had dutifully knocked the stumps into the ground in readiness for our cricket.

The boys were in a jocular mood and made one or two remarks, exceedingly rare for them, in a style that I felt was socially arrogant. Against my nature, I was stung by what I probably wrongly perceived as a sentence or two of class disparity. My eyes darted round the handsome doorway. There, in one corner, was a stirrup pump and a bucket of water. I grabbed the pump and recklessly turned the pump on them. They were soaked.

Nothing was said. They went in to change while I stood in some trepidation, ruminating on what I had just done. In the grounds of Coker Court, it was like an act of unspeakable blasphemy. I thought of my father's job at a time when there weren't many going round. I thought of Mother, recruited to don her neatly pressed black and white uniform to help lay the places for a society dinner at the Court. Above all, I thought of my own impetuous, ill-chosen words over a trifling incident that I may have misinterpreted in any case. Possibly the first hint of a complex was surfacing in me.

The brothers returned dressed in items from their Uncle Claude's wardrobe. They looked cross but not any kind of reprimand was spoken. We got on with our cricket. I can never be certain whether they harboured resentment at my upstart behaviour. Not once was our fleeting difference ever again mentioned. I don't think that their family was told. So jobs were safe.

At this distance, after all the radical political twists, some of those early divisions now seem risible, however much remnants of the old order can still be detected. I even sensed it on occasions in the cricket press box when for a moment I was confused by flashes of unfamiliar arcane public school phraseology that for an Old Etonian or two had never quite gone away. It was rare.

In honesty I continue to retain the image of Mrs Heneage waving at the estate tenants from the back-seat window of her car in suspiciously regal style, while the memory also offers its own amusing tableau of the parlour maids wiping the flour from their faces amid the flustered curtsies as the Lady of the House made one of her unscheduled arrivals below stairs.

My own acute embarrassment, in the context of the gracious Mrs Heneage, came when, among her distinguished visitors – one of many, ranging from erstwhile prime ministers, socialites and royals sharing a West Country invitation for a few days at the Badminton home of the Duke of Beaufort – she was accompanying Queen Mary on a decidedly stately early-evening stroll around the lilac laden lawns and gravel pathways of Coker Court.

Dad had wind of the Queen's visit and his whispers added drama to the unpublicised call of Royalty to East Coker. It roused my curiosity, and with youthful enterprise I went in search of what I hoped might be a more intimate view. I knew Mrs Heneage favoured evening strolls before dinner so, rather daringly, I installed myself in a high privet hedge and optimistically waited. To my surprise my patience was quickly rewarded. Around the manicured lawn and pathway came a small procession. At the head, in smiling, contemplative mood, came Mrs Heneage and the Queen of England. It was too much for me. I leaned forward to encapsulate my good fortune. Here was something to tell Vonnie, my next-door neighbour, and the boys from the village.

Already I was rehearsing the exchanges. "Don't bloody believe you."

"Yes, I bloody well did." And so on. I reckoned, well out of my parents' hearing, I could risk the odd swear word to celebrate my evening of royal patronage.

But then, suddenly, oh dear, the slender upper branches of the privet hedge snapped and I went tumbling out, onto the lawn only feet away from the decorous procession. It startled the party, although I wasn't around to discover what was said. Almost in the same movement I had gone, out through a hole in the hedge and, trembling with fear and apprehension, I was chasing down across the parkland in the vague direction of my home.

I worried about my father's future employment. I had heard the word 'trespassing' and wondered whether I might be guilty of that. And would Mrs Heneage turn the police on me? It was a dramatic, unvarnished incident, with nothing added. Even today, when I return to the village and walk across the park, I glance wistfully at the hedge from which I fell at the feet of the Queen. I have no idea whether half the estate workers were sent off to try to find me. With unbounded relief, I eventually assumed that no-one had recognised me. My dad's job was safe. I wasn't a security risk.

But before long, in the late 1940s, when what many saw as a drastic, unsentimental social and political restructuring of land ownership, the old contentious divisions were about to go for ever. It pulled me up in my more vacuous teenage moments to ponder what was happening. East Coker's estate had been picturesquely worked and maintained over its two thousand acres. Now the ten tenants were suddenly going round with sullen expressions and unseeing eyes. Major David Walker-Heneage, who had inherited the much-envied estate on the death of his mother, realistically feared it was now the end. Mournful paragraphs, formally phrased, appeared in the local papers, referring to 'the burden of death duties and taxation' and the misery of having to sell up after all those generations of family ownership.

By 1949 most of the property had been sold. Maybe it offered a morsel of consolation to me that Verandah Cottage was the last cottage to go. Dad would chat to the local farmers who didn't compromise in their expressions of grief. I heard one say: "It's a real bugger! And no proper warning. Don't know what's going to happen to us."

The disintegration of Coker Court, its fields, lilacs and wisteria, its rustic history and a simple life that shaped me with its marked dichotomy of intention, had slipped away in front of me. At the same time, despite my radical leanings, an undeniable affection had surfaced to remind me what I would now be missing.

Simon Heneage's XI
v East Coker, 1952
Ten public school boys and me in the plain white cap

5

EDUCATION AND A BEE-STING

It wouldn't be true to say that I really enjoyed my schooldays. Maybe the disciplines cut across the countryside life and the freedom of the open fields that I had come to love so much. But I did what I was told, grabbing at new knowledge that held my attention and stirred my imagination, while working harder for a few days when it was exam time.

Influenced by my parents, I behaved decently in class. I suppose you would say that my academic progress was adequate or, according to some of the teachers, encouraging. I was at least bright enough to go to grammar school, where we played rugby instead of football, and did cross-country running, through a squelchy sewerage farm, on games afternoon. We also wore at our Yeovil seat of learning a maroon blazer with a Latin motto. Dear old East Coker council school was left a little behind in the process.

*My first day at school
in the jersey knitted by my mother*

I experienced three headmasters – contrasting markedly in physique, temperament and attitude to the job. At my village school, Mr Murley, William Ewart I remember, was in charge. He was quite thick-set and had come through the horrors of the 1914-18 war. They may have contributed to strong, stubborn views and political thoughts that veered to the left. He was a heavy smoker, mostly Goldflakes, and the smell of strong tobacco clung to his suit. His voice carried unequivocal authority; he kept a cane and ensured its presence remained visible in a high cupboard, over a pile of faded text-books. I was caned twice, which was considered a badge of inordinate honour among my young classmates. The three swishes, two of them on the right hand were symbols of practised venom. My fingers swelled and the sight of them was requested and admired at break-time. The first offence, involving from me an unconventional way of conveying the answer to an exam teaser in mental arithmetic, was for an ingenious though trifling misdemeanour. The second classroom felony was complicated and mystifying to me. It became something of an inexhaustible talking point among my wide-eyed young contemporaries.

Mr Murley was a practical man. He wanted his pupils to do well. In the same way, he wanted the boys to turn into good husbands, who knew how to dig the garden – the school had its own allotment – or make honey from their own bees. The head was proud of his bees and the hives were out of bounds except for the favoured few who were allowed to put on veils and examine the hives. One Friday afternoon, I ventured too close and was quite badly stung on the head. It needed attention and I was taken to Miss Wilcox, the deputy head, for treatment. The incident became a major talking point, far more absorbing than the period of technical drawing that Mr Murley had recently introduced to the teaching syllabus. He discovered what had happened and, for a reason that I found hard to understand, went into a furious rage. It left me flustered – as if the bee sting wasn't bad enough. What the devil was I doing, daring to go near his bee hives, he demanded? A throbbing skull caused me unwisely to bluff it out. "Don't know, sir, I woke with a headache this morning. Wasn't a sting, sir." It was a pathetic and needless attempt to offer an alternative reason for taking on a colony of fractious bees. I can still see him stubbing out his Goldflake on a brick wall as doubtless he contemplated the loss of a fine worker bee.

"So you lie as well. No pupil of mine will ever lie." With a minimum of public rebuke from that point, he frog-marched me into his cramped office, stretching up for that infamous, torturous weapon of excessive classroom punishment and injustice. Three more murderous swishes. Three more swollen fingers. "Now get back to your room." This time I did a diversion and went into the lavatory. And, very privately, I cried. But, my goodness, it hurt. Bloody bees!

That was Mr Murley. It's possible that he saw too much cruelty during the war. He certainly advocated a Spartan approach to our schooling. Most mornings, including those in mid-winter, he had us out in the playground, doing a strict rotation of physical jerks. Pullovers off. Noses blue with the cold. He supervised the exercises himself. Part of the regular, unsparing routine involved deep breathing. In and out, in and out. He was convinced that it was the perfect antidote for wheezy chests and other signs of suspect health. As far as I recall, it wasn't wholeheartedly shared by his shivering pupils.

My second headmaster – by this time I was at the grammar school – was JW Pearson, another martinet who cut an intimidating figure with his withering look guaranteed to quell the faintest suggestion of rebellious youth. He had a glass eye which added to his rather fearsome appearance. Everyone agreed, at least after he had completed his 22 years at the school, that he was a brilliant, innovative head. Some of his academic philosophies were those of a Victorian. At morning assembly his voice was there to be heard, whether in the hymns or any reprimands about wayward standards. He surprised many of us, after retirement, by being ordained and taking over a country parish.

The third head, Denys Thompson, was to me by some distance the most influential and fascinating. His lucidly written books on the purer use of English and the subject's place in the secondary curriculum were of lasting value. In the thirties he had written with FR Leavis. As a teacher he made an unquestionable, quiet-voiced impact, with Auden among his pupils. At Yeovil School, where he remained in charge from 1944 to 1962, he took an unfussy satisfaction in the record number of boys who went on to Oxbridge. He was acknowledged as an outstanding literary figure and editor.

When I left school at 16, he suppressed his horror, no doubt, when I told him that I was hoping for some kind of career in journalism. He wasn't much taken by the standards and tendencies of the tabloids or what he saw as the manner in which political and social news was fictionalised and manipulated. He may have assumed I wanted to go on to university instead. In fact, such a progression had never entered my head. For the most part it just didn't occur to village boys and girls. He was the most unassuming of men, happier writing his academic articles, I imagine, than self-consciously delivering words of warning at assembly about what would happen to boys caught smoking over the lunch break.

Apart from my brief farewell handshake and his kindly good wishes as I moved off into the world of weekly paper clichés, we had barely exchanged a sentence during my days in the fifth and sixth form at school. So I was much surprised when he remembered me, years later, on the evening we both attended an old boys' dinner. Even better, and more surprising, he wanted to talk cricket.

Fawningly I told him that I had several of his books. He flattered me by asking for one of mine. It led to a warm exchange of letters. His handwriting was just as I recalled it from my school reports. The content of his letters was blissfully not laden with school reminiscences or the names of former boys who had achieved some status though now meaning little to either of us. "I bet you didn't know how much I like cricket," he wrote. "I used to love watching Kent. Frank Woolley was my favourite." The effortless, embracing handwritten vignette that followed was a long way from some of those slightly stuffy essays that Denys Thompson prepared for literature conferences. It had a boyish charm. We shared our unaffected enthusiasm for the game. It was never headmaster and pupil. We were jointly enraptured by memories of square cuts. There was not one mention of a subordinate clause.

School for me has rarely been a place for stifling learning. At East Coker, in a building which always seemed cold, making us long for more coke in the old-fashioned stove, Miss Wilcox was a gifted teacher. She was too strict for some, yet she had time to guide her subject beyond the strictures of the approved text books. She warned us of the dangers of ringworm and advised us to sneeze into a handkerchief. She devoted half a lesson to showing us, naïve as we were, the proper way to brush our teeth or how to take care over our appearances. I think she'd have liked children of her own. Miss Wilcox lived contentedly in the village, overlooking one of Coker Court's parks, for half a century. I have every reason to be grateful for the painless way she imparted knowledge – and the sherry trifles she gave my parents for Christmas. Her one concession to mild eccentricity was her enthusiasm for donkeys. She lovingly looked after several, encouraging them to come virtually up to her back door.

Growing up in the village was for me a variegated joy. Like most of my school mates, I broke the mile-long journey home by persuading the blacksmith to let me blow the bellows and tenderly pat the weary old cart horse. Mr Murley, who must have seen a likeable side in me, let me play the toy drum in the percussion band, some sort of musical advancement on the triangle.

But the head was inclined to be mean when it came to games afternoon. He had two sets of football kit but to my knowledge they were never washed. The stench of dried mud and worse made the point. All the time I was at the school, we didn't play any kind of improvised football match more than three or four times. And I scored twice. This was an accomplishment I record only because I must have been the slowest – and perhaps the chubbiest – player on the field. My uncharacteristic triumphs could still be recounted today in detail by me. Do we really hang on to small-boy success with such unmitigated pleasure? In a stinking shirt, too?

Then it was on to grammar school, something that pleased my parents. From a small class seven of us passed our scholarships. It was a marvellous statistic. Only years later did we realise the extent of the academic drive from Miss Wilcox and Mr Murley. Teaching methods had been conventional with no fancy tricks of tuition. I thought at least two others from my year also deserved to go to grammar school. Life wasn't always fair.

My opening day there, in a new building only recently opened, carried personal drama. I had a new bike for the daily journey of four miles and my parents had asked another, older boy to accompany me. I wasn't used to busy roads but was travelling cautiously when a big car, going too fast, overtook me, clipping my right handlebar. I was thrown into the road where a crowd quickly gathered. The driver of the big car pulled in and walked back. My first concern was for my spanking £4 bike. It seemed none the worse for the collision; nor was I. I wasn't quite sure what to do. So I mumbled an apology and, still trembling, eventually resumed my journey.

What I do remember, at this distance, is the conflicting evidence. "Silly young bugger. Shouldn't be on the road."

And from another onlooker: "Not the kid's fault. I blame the driver."

There were no notes and addresses exchanged. The varying dialogue can be heard every day at road accidents. We see crashes from different angles, with different prejudices. Our eyes let us down. We draw conclusions too easily. How reliable are the witnesses?

My 8 a.m. accident, on the West Coker Road not far from the Quicksilver Mail inn, left no injuries on the body, no scratches on that big car, no blasphemies from the portly, neatly suited driver as far as I could tell. If there were murmurs under his breath as he climbed back into his well-padded driver's seat, I didn't hear them.

As I set off a second time, my companion gave me an odd look. "That was a good start for you in a new school. Know who it was?"

I shook my head. "Well, that bloke in the swish car was the chairman of the governors at Yeovil School … Alderman WJC Pittard."

It could have been worse but the accident was still in its way spectacular. I suppose you could say the years that followed, in my grammar school education, were unspectacular. All that cycling, to and from Mudford Road, made me slimmer. In my form of 30 were some high-fliers, boys heading for Oxford and Cambridge. But I always ended the term in the top six or seven. I got into the cricket XI and stayed there for two years, batting with an undistinguished flair and deceptively flamboyant cover drive at six or seven in the order.

Yeovil Grammar School cricket team
I am standing, fourth from right

My English master, Darral Wood, who was also in charge of cricket, had promoted me on the strength of a few innings, bolstered by those off drives, in a house match when I opened the batting and bowling. I think I must have been a let-down for Darral, someone who brought English literature alive and regularly gave me an uplifting mark for my essays. Years later I met him again and thanked him for the encouragement he showed me in my study of Conrad, then a set book, and my cricket. He had an appreciation for the sound of language. "Did I really? Put it down to alliteration." In truth, without knowing it, however, he had ensured that English would always be my favourite subject – and would lead indirectly to my career in newspapers. Not that Shakespeare with his alien cadencies meant much to me. I liked the word rhythms rather than the complicated plots. When we did Lear in class, I was given Edmund, the bastard, to read aloud. As for the Shakespearean comedies, I hated most of them.

But the standard of teaching varied a great deal during the wartime years. 'Taffy' Rees, who took French, was one of the best. But he was a strange, solitary individual who wore open-neck shirts and sandals during much of the year. He was a Quaker and, I frequently fancied, had too many deep-seated phobias and traces of a fearful inferiority complex. It was something that operated in an irritating, inverted way.

There was the time I was sent to the Staff Room during the lunch-hour with a message for Mr 'Tich' Palmer, who took us for rugby and occasionally basic horticulture. I knocked gingerly on the staff door and Taffy opened it. Rarely blessed with abundant self-confidence, and now darting a nervous glace into the teachers' cavern where the occupants read the morning paper or shared a cigarette, the abstemious Mr Rees awaited my request.

"Please sir, can I have a word with Mr Palmer?" It apparently didn't come out quite like that. My West Country accent was pronounced in those days. It sounded more like I wanted to speak to Mr Pawmurr. Taffy paused, clearly enjoying my discomfiture. He had no great sense of humour but now his lips curled into a dry smile. He turned back to his fellow teachers. "Mr Pawmurr," he mocked. "This boy would like a word with you." Then, as if to lengthen his personal joke at my expense, he addressed no one in particular: "That is if we've got a Mr-em-Pawmurr on the staff."

Taffy was being singularly insensitive, and I'm sure the Society of Friends wouldn't have approved of this needless episode when one of his own social hang-ups was not far from the surface. He'd gone out of his way openly to humiliate me because of my village-boy burr. It was slighting and hurtful. He continued to give me high marks for French but I never forgave him. On my opening day at grammar school, he had each boy telling him, in faltering French, what his father did for a living. He was, I assume, determining the social pecking order.

I made firm friends from within my form, not for a moment envious that some of them would be off to university. We cycled partly home together after school, gossiping like old women as they pegged their clothes and exchanged choice snippets from neighbouring washing lines. Our conversation got spiced by salacious whispers we had eagerly picked up. We were now potential adults after all.

My education, not wholly gleaned from the bookish demands of the classroom, was expanding at a rapid rate. The hormones were beginning to nag away. I wanted a first girl friend but hadn't found one yet. And I wanted to leave school, even though I had no idea what I would do for a living. The acne bothered me as it did so many wartime schoolboys.

I used to lie in my small bedroom and wonder about my future. Verandah Cottage, a listed building and centuries old, had been my rock. As for my educational reflections, I was convinced that the village pub just across the road, had – especially in the earlier years – been my most effective academy of learning. I used to lean out from the front bedroom window and, at closing time, would crane to catch the words of intimacy being exchanged, the hushed invites, the fumbled guilty kisses, the cruder fragments of carnal intent. This was where I learned so much about life, its transgressions and bodily excitement. I was an avid listener and learner.

It was in the village pub, then still called the New Inn, that I watched the tragic decline of Ivan Guinness, generally believed to be the likely heir to a family fortune. In my teenage days of human discovery and wide, wondering eyes, I'd see him and his young wife arrive soon after opening time. Some days I would join them, in my inquisitive, eavesdropping way, in the otherwise deserted bar. Guinness was, everyone told me, a drunk beyond recovery. He slurred his words even in mid-morning. Once or twice he brought me into the conversation, though his staccato, inconsequential words lacked meaning or context. He may have warmed to an under-age drinker with the glass of lemonade I pretended was scrumpy.

I was aware that his family, with its share of misfortune, was both well known and well heeled. That boosted my interest. I noticed that his measures were never singles. I had read about lush life styles, but he was the first drunk I had ever seen at close, unsteady quarters. In a matter of weeks he was dead – from heart failure under an anaesthetic while having a tooth out. The inquest confirmed that he was a chronic alcoholic and that his liver was almost completely destroyed. The tall, wan son of Sir Arthur Guinness, who went through the motions of running a smallholding in East Coker, was dead at the age of 29. Yes, the pub was truly my classroom in diverse life.

How will I ever forget the morning during the war when a small crowd of boys found something we at first thought was a balloon, hanging on my grandfather's front gate. I knew for certain it had not been his. We discussed its purpose with the intensity of a group of natural history pundits. Then one of our youthful party surprised the rest of us by announcing with some hitherto undisclosed authority: "Hure, you know what that is, don't you? It's a bloomin' French letter."

To be honest, that didn't help many of us. I was as confused as the rest. "A letter? Not even wrapped up for posting?" Our knowledgeable mate explained as the rest of us stood in rapt silence. There followed a collective gasp. "They calls it a frenchie. Stops you havin' kids."

Pete, the Informer, went up considerably in our estimation. After that, all of us were apt to talk glibly in our own kind of schoolboy sophistication about French letters – the sort you didn't put in the post. We were growing up.

The window from which I learned so much

6

NEARLY A LIBEL ACTION

So why journalism? It wasn't as if I knew much about it, apart from the belief that all the Sunday paper reporters wore trilbies at rakish angles like the *People*'s Arthur Helliwell and they dispensed a rich seam of human interest. I was by this time becoming an incorrigible newspaper reader, envying some of those Fleet Street practitioners with their racy styles – short sentences, dramatic narrative and a staggering range of subject matter. I was gradually becoming seduced, whether I was aware of it or not, by that maligned profession's sheer mystique. But I had no idea how I might get started.

My grammar school progress had tapered off and I had no intention of staying another year in the sixth form, simply so that I could convince the patient Darral Wood I really was capable of making runs from the lower middle order or turning the ball from the off if only I was given more of a chance. I had already drifted away gratefully from the sciences. English, the use of words which didn't have to be long or pretentious, remained my favourite pursuit at school. "How about teaching English?" one master suggested. No thanks, I told myself, altogether too sedentary. Where was the romance in that?

Yeovil had a weekly paper, one of the oldest in the country, the *Western Gazette*. It was painfully staid, with advertisements monopolising the front page, seeming to me to specialise in cattle markets, obituaries, paying too much homage to the regional plutocrats and making sure it didn't upset the advertisers. The coverage over a number of counties was wonderfully comprehensive. Every parish council meeting, every Women's Institute revolutionary departure in jam-making, every stodgy lecture of the local Rotarians was dutifully reported. On reflection I'm not certain how they found the space to squeeze in any serious rural polemics. It was a lesson in logistics, sorting out all the varying editions. The formula appeared infallible in maintaining a healthy circulation. The constant success of the *Western Gazette* was then the envy of other regional weekly papers. Not that you found many Arthur Helliwells on their reporting staffs.

But if I wanted to call myself a journalist, and was prepared to hang around in search of that nebulous status, it was my only obvious route. I put on my ill-fitting serge suit, propped my bike against the side of the building and arranged to see the managing director. "No, young man. We have no vacancies for a copy boy. Ring us again in a few months' time." I did, a number of times. As for my uncertain future as a proper journalist, I at least continued going into the Corporation's reading room every evening to check how the different national papers dealt with the same story, mentally writing my own version of the latest crime of passion. I drooled over the more salacious accounts and suspected I already knew what sold papers. Just for balance, I also liked to dip into the erudite pages of the *New Statesman* and *The Spectator*. It was a kind of sub-conscious concession to Denys Thompson.

After a succession of phone calls to the managing director's secretary, I was told that the present copy boy, 'Buzz' Fenner, was being promoted and I could have his job. My parents weren't quite sure what to make of it. My grandfather, who had intently watched my indeterminate progress and only wanted me to become a motor mechanic, scraped out his briar without comment. "Perhaps you can work for the *News Chronicle*," he eventually said. "No, just the *Western Gazette*," was my sheepish reply.

My journalistic apprenticeship was a pallid one. I pulled proofs, ran incessant errands for the sub-editors, opened the editorial mail and answered the phone. On Mondays and Thursdays, when there were news envelopes to be collected at the Town station, my work started at 6.30 a.m. That was after my cycle ride from East Coker. I know I exasperated Harry Lanham, the assistant editor, with my time-keeping record. In a few cases, there was a valid excuse. At the height of windy winter, my brown trilby once came off as I freewheeled at some speed down Hendford Hill. It ended up on the single-track railway line. Still half asleep and not naturally athletic, I slid down the steep embankment and, with difficulty, made my Alpine ascent back to the roadway. By the time I got to the office, caked in mud, one of the displeased sub-editors had collected the news parcels himself from the station. I don't think my explanation for late arrival was believed. Precariously I blustered my apologies and kept my job.

There were several young reporters and, as I so often found in those early years, life in a claustrophobic newspaper office was unfailingly companionable. We went drinking together, gulping down black-and-tans as if we were already established Fleet Street boozers. We pretended we were louche and a bit decadent, proper writers, when we were really still embarrassingly gauche, in our small-town unworldliness. What we shared was a congenial nature, and an eagerness to swap local stories and rumours about Town Hall officials, felonious police officers who liked literally to get out of uniform, and self-important shopkeepers of Masonic persuasion whose lodge meetings were too convenient a supposed reason to hide furtive dalliances from their wives.

At the *Gazette*, newspaper tuition was really minimal. It was assumed that no-one would ever want to leave the paper. Those in authority were kindly and benevolent, while intolerant of any glimmer of literary enterprise Every news story was a parody of the last one – in style and phraseology. Any tentative flight of imagination was instantly condemned and spiked. "Now let's see, that was a nice write-up of yours on the county court case, young David. Took no liberties with the evidence. Your shorthand must be coming along. We must give you a few more courts to cover. The trouble is we have to be so careful. No-one ever sues the *Western Gazette* for an inaccuracy, you know."

"I'm sure that is so, Mr Lanham." By this time I had gained enough self-confidence, still not too much, to slip in a gentle slither of sarcasm. Mr Lanham, in his blue suit and with his demeanour of non-conformist, non-contentious goodness, saw my throwaway as nothing but confirmation of the paper's worthiness.

Above all, we were taught the virtue of accuracy. Length was discussed in 'sticks', not columns. If we were reporting the local Tory's speech at the Party's summer fayre, we were asked for six sticks of copy, and that was what was delivered. At a funeral service – and I attended so many of them that I tended to dream of coffins rather than goalposts – it was not enough to get the Brigadier's surname and rank right; it was obligatory for me to check and re-check the ex-military man's three initials, in the right order. Far too often, I stood in church porches, the rain pouring off the brim of my brown trilby, as I was patronised by a dignitary who thought I should know his name without having to ask for it. Was he, in his view, more important than the deceased?

My seven years at the *Gazette* taught me so much about human nature. It ensured that I would remain in life an unshakable egalitarian. It also demonstrated the weakness of a paper or one of its reporters being too deferential. That has nothing at all to do with bad manners or misplaced aggression. It is a measure of self-esteem and human dignity.

I had no regrets about working at this newspaper. It just went on too long and there was no encouragement if a reporter occasionally stretched himself with a decent image and dared to tiptoe beyond the accepted literary parameters.

We weren't paid very well but the paper sent us off in turn to learn shorthand – in a little living room where an over-fed ginger cat sprawled across the table, giving us hay fever as well as a spattering of Pitman's artistic and now almost redundant hieroglyphics. We were reimbursed, too, for driving lessons. To celebrate my pass, at the second attempt, I crept into the front office and asked Shirley, someone I had lusted after for weeks on account of her fabulous and much envied breasts, whether I could drive her home for lunch. I reported, with the grandest of gestures, in the office car at 1 p.m. Shirley had touched up her luscious lips, I remember. I sat her in beside me – and in a matter of seconds I drove straight into the parked van in front of us. I looked at her; she had a scintilla of glass decorously balancing on her nose. Otherwise there were no injuries, apart from a buckled office car which I knew I would have to explain.

We exchanged wry looks and from the comely Shirley a brave attempt at a laugh. "Better scrub the lift. Em, the clutch was a bit fierce. Sorry about that."

She extricated herself from the passenger seat. I was too preoccupied to appreciate the sensual movement of her shapely bronzed legs. "Maybe another time. But a nice thought." And she was gone, dabbing her unbloodied nose. I never had another chance to take her out for a ride on stolen time.

The three or four of us from the cramped Reporters' Room had a convivial time. Donald, our senior colleague by a few years, shared our humour. He had a manic Michael Bentine laugh and ended up the paper's personable editor. He had an extrovert nature and used to drive round Dorset's muddy, winding lanes on a motor bike. 'Buzz' Fenner was a voracious reader who defiantly refused later to have a television set. As a teenager and after, he was renowned for his lubricious inclinations. He operated sexually in the plural and kept us engrossed with the graphic reports that followed. As a group we trusted each other implicitly. Indiscretions were colourfully varied and we made certain they were kept in-house (whoever's house that might be). Our group was completed by Durban Frost, who covered classical music from his own days as a cub reporter. He went on to work for the *Guardian* (he beat me on the short list for one West Country-based post) and then worked in London and abroad for BBC radio. He had numerous roles, covering among them farming and for a time royal affairs. Three of us – Fenner, Frost and Foot – remained close. We savoured the same memories. More than sixty years later we were still having pub lunches together, sometimes talking like grumbling old men as we deplored the way journalism had gone. Conversation was never a problem. It was only, we observed, that we found ourselves talking less about sex and more about the war in Afghanistan as we matured. But the bond, and with it the nostalgic chuckles, remained.

Fenner, Frost and Foot

The *Gazette* actively discouraged us from supplementing our meagre wages by doing any surreptitious work for rival papers. My employers just didn't acknowledge their own parsimony. "We don't want you doing anything for them, young David. Their writing styles would get you into bad habits. They take chances with the facts. And, after all, you're paid to work for us. Just think of your prospects by staying with us." The logic of that argument didn't much impress us. In my case, the distinct possibility of ending up as the Langport or Crewkerne district man, sitting in the corner of the bar – as Bill Diamond ritualistically, loyally did – waiting for the local club secretaries to drop in with their local weekly news items, bore no resemblance at all to my lurking Fleet Street concept of rolling presses.

But of course we needed additional work from somewhere. As a prop forward of negligible mobility and shove, who in house matches at school paradoxically took the place kicks, I was enlisted to be the *Gazette*'s rugby correspondent. I got to know all the players well. There was a bank manager, an insurance executive who was a smooth charmer off the field and a maniacal physical brute from the murky depths of the scrum, a pub landlord and my dentist who lacked as much subtlety chasing for the line as he did with menacing instruments in the surgery. They invited me to share their jugs of ale after the game. In return, I gave them all glowing write-ups and on occasions, to please the rest of the team, bestowed in print a fictitious, impeccably conceived try on a player who usually missed such public acclaim. The readers never found out.

Rugby also carried financial reward. I found myself writing short accounts of Yeovil RFC's matches for up to half a dozen national papers – at five shillings a time. The club treasurer had quite an elevated position in one of the high street banks. He was in charge of the office's security key at the weekends, and would let me in by a side door so that I could use the bank's phone. The treasurer was delighted that his side of hybrid occupations and suspect rugby skills was deemed worthy of mention in several Sunday national papers. It was for me a civilised way to dictate my reports, in this silent, empty strangely eerie bank, and was never remotely repeated in such comfort during my hundreds of rugby and football dictated accounts that followed. I suppose it was the nearest I ever got to studying the mentality of a bank robber.

The news pages of the more lurid Sunday papers continued to absorb me. Nominally I knew all the famous by-liners and wondered whether one day I might meet Duncan Webb, who wrote fearlessly about the Messina brothers and Soho's square mile of vice. I could reel off the names of all the gang leaders, not to mention the convicted brothel keepers and the pretty, painted girls with respectable suburban parents who themselves made lucrative livings as vicarious dance hostesses before flogging their titillating tales to an over-receptive EC4.

While still a junior reporter, peddling the council meetings and the funeral reports regularly of 600 or more mourners' names, I experienced my first libel action, even though it was eventually settled out of court, coinciding with a front-page apology that was as long as the original story. I'd picked up the bones of a gentle romance that had been regenerated after fifty years. In the meantime the couple, one linked to a bakery firm in Yeovil, had lost contact and married elsewhere. The husband had actually gone to live in America. Now, with their respective partners dead, the two had chanced to meet up again. The one-time sweethearts decided to get married.

I confided in my colleagues. "Bloody good story, Dave. Loads of human interest. Make sure you offer it to a national before someone else does." Already I had that in mind. "Think I'll try the *People*. Right up their street." Dutifully I wrote a short version for the *Gazette*. To my surprise, this example of rather flat prose got into the *Gazette* virtually untouched. It earned me muted praise from the weekly's hierarchy.

What I didn't want now was for some young chancer on one of Yeovil's three evening papers to dress up the story and beat me to a nice little moonlighting earner. So I wasted no time dictating my piece, breezily written in short sentences and with even a good-natured innuendo, to the *People*. The response was instant. "Like it, old boy. Just needs a few more quotes. Bit of sex, you know."

Well frankly, I wasn't too sure. We didn't deal in sex, not even the most wholesome kind, on the *Gazette*. Carefully, perhaps daringly for me, after taking another look at my notebook, I lengthened, or should I say invented, the potential husband's observations. They were innocuous after all. I gave the impression that I had gone to talk to him a second time.

From that point, my enterprise became fraught with dangers. The *People* had my office number and they kept ringing me. By then all the sub-editorial staff were caught up in the drama as well as my acute embarrassment. "What's this, son? Writing for another paper. Going to take some explaining." The *People* came out first. The story was on the front page under the headline FIFTY YEARS OF LOST LOVE. The sexual nuance was there for all to read, especially by an introvert geriatric couple whose walls were plastered with religious tracts. The racy opening paragraph informed the readers that the reunion had been celebrated with raised champagne glasses. And they were, I knew, unshakable teetotallers.

My reaction was an amalgam of emotions. I didn't remotely recognise the story as the one I had originally sent the London paper. The numerous quotes were unmitigated fiction, although not overtly defamatory or upbeat. I couldn't bear to imagine how the couple would be feeling. They'd be citing me as the only reporter who had spoken to them. Would there be legal repercussions? I was still in the church choir, mainly to please my parents, but my modest bass voice was even more subdued then usual. The story's publication, at the same time, gave me a surge of journalistic new boy's pleasure and pride. The other reporters complimented me and told me they didn't realise I could churn out a human-interest tale like that. So I was reluctant to tell them about the imbalance of fiction.

The retraction was fulsome. I think I counted eleven facts that the story got wrong. In the week that elapsed after the published front-page account, the poor couple were visited by intrusive fellow journalists; they found themselves as wretched celebrities, tired of saying with some fury that they had nothing to add to "this tale of lies". They had employed a firm of solicitors who were inundating the *People* with phone calls by the Tuesday morning. The smooth-talking newsdesk man who had deftly liaised with me – and taken such liberties – the previous week was back again. "Don't worry about it, old boy. No, it won't go to court. Our lawyers will sort that out. Just like you to do one thing for me. Can you send us your notes from the interviews and, well, make or two minor changes?"

That was something I hadn't expected. The good-natured fiction was one thing and didn't too seriously challenge my sense of morality. But being asked to revise my notes, making them more favourable to the *People*, was something else. That did trouble me and I was grateful not to be asked for any doctored account a second time.

I was a raw junior reporter and squirmed for a month or two. It was a lesson in a popular national paper's attitudes, ephemeral concerns of misconduct and an adept facility to shift any blame from themselves back onto a manipulated journo from the sticks.

Nothing more was said to me about my wavering judgement from the *Gazette*'s more sanctimonious heights. But apart from those few days of fleeting excitement – and temerity – was the dalliance with Fleet Street really worth it?

The answer must be no. My cheque from the *People* followed at the end of the month. It came to three guineas.

The *Western Gazette* building reminded me of a hospital. It was sturdy and reliable. It had lengthy corridors and I sometimes felt the numerous doors on either side led into one-gender wards. The girls, with their traditional sing-song voices as they checked the small ads, crowded round a big table in the Readers' Room. The men, eager for their permitted time to roll a cigarette or take a pinch of snuff, tended their machines with traditional affection. They monopolised the Composing Room where there was the whiff of printers' ink and freshly minted words in silver.

I, too, was captivated by the human warmth and aged aura but was ready to move on. At the *Gazette*, amid its many accepted virtues, no editorial was too boring, no word too long, no front page of advertisement any different visually from the previous year (or generation, we sometimes thought). "Don't try any of that silly, fancy writing, David, and you can be here for life." In fact, the next week I was gone.

Yet another picturesque phrase had been stifled. Two letters of minor complaint had also come in, objecting to the way I had described a nondescript Gilbert and Sullivan production (they should have sent Durban who at least knew what he was talking about). I was tired of having to cycle all the way up Babylon Hill, kit tied to the crossbars, to play cricket for the *Gazette* cricket club. Most of us were in no physical state to field in the Compton House buttercups when we got to the ground. That was a pity. We had an attractive away fixture list, too, playing against Devon players of Minor Counties rank. Our side included one or two fine players, like Derek Blanchard, nicknamed The Strangler, the Geoff Boycott of West Country club cricket. He had dogmatic views and often excelled as an all-rounder in compensation.

But I'd had enough. I was due a Friday off and took the bus to Bristol before impulsively stepping into the lift for the editorial department of the *Evening World*, part of the Northcliffe chain of brash provincials and despised, I have no doubt, by the varied editors and executives of my weekly. I had no plan, apart from seeking a new job where fewer clichés and more breezy writing were encouraged. I hadn't even told my parents of my logistical gamble. I had a vague idea there might be a vacancy for a cricket writer on the *World* to take over from Ron Roberts – later to manage overseas tours – but George Baker, the most delightful of sports editors, told me it was filled.

As I walked dispiritedly out of the room, the news editor called me back. "Fancy a job on the news side?" Formalities were cursory; the *Evening World* probably had no budget any longer to advertise nationally for staff so I saved them a few bob. It was all arranged in five minutes. Now it was a matter of hitching lifts back to East Coker, warily telling Mum and Dad that I was leaving them shortly, and handing in my notice. The latter wasn't as difficult as I'd expected. Suddenly I was consumed with a feeling of freedom and adventure. In a perverse way I'd enjoyed the weekly's enforced chores and restrictions, even when standing in dozens of church doorways to take mourners' names. But now, as I saw it, I was about to become … a proper journalist. I was halfway to Fleet Street.

7

NATIONAL SERVICE

I resented my National Service. It interrupted the pattern of my private newspaper aspirations and, even before I reported to Padgate to collect my ill-fitting RAF uniform, I envisaged my next two years as a criminal waste of time and government money. I made friends, however, harboured unrealistic hopes of becoming a spy during those frigid months of the Cold War and actually came frighteningly close to murdering a malevolent drill instructor.

Maybe in the shaping of my village-boy personality I was ready to leave home for the first time. My parents didn't say too much. They suppressed as usual any outward indications of emotion. "Who's going to dig the early tiddies now?" my dad joked. Mother was more concerned that I'd be wearing damp shirts on their return from the RAF laundry. They realised I wasn't a practical person and wondered aloud whether I'd be able to manage the necessities of life without the present maternal guidance.

The reluctant National Serviceman

It seemed to me that I should, as compensation, treat National Service as a bit of an adventure. At least I was a good mixer. I was also in reasonable health and had peed with reassuring masculine vigour at my medical when self-conscious fellow recruits struggled to operate their bladders at full capacity. That gave me a heartening psychological boost on my journey to enforced conscription and restricted freedom.

At Padgate I discovered that Fred Trueman had been among the previous 'intake' and that Blackpool's Jackie Mudie was already ensconced in his new uniform. The tailor fitted me out with no more than token regard for my shape. A bundle of uniform was slapped in front of each of us and we struggled out into the brisk Lancashire air to await news of our first posting. Mine was Hereford, then an increasingly run-down square-bashing camp.

I'd applied for the RAF because I'd been told, quite erroneously as it turned out, that this Service offered by some distance the gentlest introduction to the parade-ground disciplines that I was about to face. The reality was indescribably savage. I can only imagine that the drill instructors, corporals with granite faces and the glint of sadism in everything they barked at us to do, had already been ditched by some evil army boot camp. They hated us as National Servicemen because many of us had come from grammar school or even in some cases higher academic echelons. The drill instructors made no attempt to disguise their contempt for us; there was inferiority complex in every expletive-strewn insult they threw at us.

They liked to pick on someone who clearly wasn't fitted for either the uniform or the physical excesses of the parade ground. Because I had completed my indentures before being conscripted, I was a year older than most of the sprogs. I never captured successfully the knack of wedging my forage cap behind my right ear. Nor was the beret that replaced it any nearer making me look like a proper airman under training. More accurately I saw myself as an abused infantryman.

"I thought people joined the RAF to fly planes, not be chased all over the bloody square," I suggested one evening with a curl of my lips to suggest appropriate sick humour.

"Oh you did, did you?" And I honestly hadn't seen the flight lieutenant in the doorway of our billet. His tone changed. "What's your number and where's your bed space? And stand to attention when I'm addressing you. Corporal, make sure this slovenly recruit is given extra duties. Just look at that bed of his. Get him making the blankets properly." The big, burly creep of a corporal, who had also just appeared, clicked his heels with exaggerated gunfire precision. And the officer advanced on my bed, pulled out all the sheets and blankets, hurling them onto the floor. "Now make it all again. When he has finished, I want you, corporal, to kick it all on the floor – and this excuse for an airman can make it a third time." With that, the officer went striding out.

The corporal, in charge of our billet, now turned on me. "You heard what the officer said. He said you were a slovenly shithouse. What did he say?"

There was no chance of any kind of a civilised debate. As I quickly discovered, there never was as a humiliated recruit in the Services. The corporal's voice bellowed again: "What did he say you were?"

With brain-dead obedience, because it was pointless and fraught with retribution if I failed to do so, I listlessly recited: "He said I was a slovenly shit. But, corporal, he didn't call me a shithouse."

"No, but I do. Another of those clever dicks from grammar school, I suppose. I've got it in for you. Let's see, 2528404. You won't think you're a clever bastard when I've finished with you."

And he meant it. For the rest of my eight weeks at Hereford he saved his unmitigated bile for me. I did my best on the parade ground but he faulted it. He needed a victim, especially if it was someone who had done rather better at school and who'd never quite got the hang of wearing his beret at the right angle. The corporal wore his like a guardsman.

I don't know what the official policy was when it came to instilling discipline. He gave us all a rough time. He had us sweeping our bed spaces with zombie zeal. The stove shone through the coal dust. Our cupboards were subjected to a daily inspection, with clean shirts, working and ceremonial uniform, boots and shoes, shaving kit, great coats all in approved order.

The corporal, who possibly came to Hereford by way of the army, liked showing off with a rifle. Quite apart from being out on the square, screaming his orders, he had us marching with those heavy rifles in the billet. We were exhausted by early evening, after being up since long before six o'clock. But he had the egregious habit of switching on all the lights for so-called supplementary drill in the middle of the night.

It was between three and half past that he stumbled into his cubicle, knocking over his sparse furniture and waking all the occupants of the billet. He'd been drinking. Having put on the lights, he addressed us in a voice that increased in decibels. "Right, you lazy buggers. We'll have a drill session." Looking straight at me as he advanced menacingly towards us, he said: "And this ass-hole, Foot, will show you how it's done. Won't you, Aircraftsman Second Class? Get out of bed when I'm talking to you – and stand to attention."

In a state of abject weariness, I mumbled a reply. "And say 'Yes, corporal'." This I did in mindless obedience.

"By yer bloody beds, all of you." Bleary-eyed, half conscious, we stood in drooping submission alongside our disturbed blankets. What was coming next?

"I've got a nice little treat lined up for smart-ass Foot." If he only knew, I'd never been a smart-ass in my life. I did my arms drill none too efficiently but as well as I could. I loathed the corporal because he went out of his way to mock my attempts to give a passing imitation of a wretched National Serviceman doing his best for King and country in a temperamentally alien environment.

What followed was a fiendish exercise dreamed up by a perverse and drunken drill instructor in the middle of the night. With that heavy rifle, he had me sloping arms and then, from a crouching position and legs giving way, ordering me to move round the four sides of the billet. The pain was excruciating and in the end I collapsed in a disabled heap. It was for him a matter of amusement, laden with cruel sadism. As a final coup de grace, he stuck his face – and beer fumes – to within inches of mine. "Enjoy that, did you? You slovenly bastard."

Suddenly I was consumed, for the only time in my life, with a sensation of overpowering evil intent. For perhaps twenty seconds or so I was out of control. I was still gripping the rifle and I wanted to bring it down against the corporal's grinning, inhuman head. I would have killed him, and nearly did. I was shaking with an intensity that deflected me from any kind of logic or restraint. In those terrifying twenty seconds, goaded beyond endurance, I had discovered the frightening proximity of life and death. I have no idea whether I would have been forgiven partially in a court of law but the incident gave me a macabre insight into the impulsive taking of another person's life. I recall it here because I have not exaggerated or fictionalised it in any way. It remains a gnawing memory of an ugly, understandable loss of control and civilised behaviour that has never quite gone away. The thought of it still frightens me.

From what I heard of other square-bashing centres, Hereford was not for the weak-hearted. Maybe I was just unlucky with the instructor; some of the others were certainly endowed with a more compassionate nature. I got the impression that a handful of rogue drill instructors competed in reputation for tyrannical variations on their personalised systems for breaking the recruits' spirits. Just once, I shamefully admit, I phoned my mother and failed to suppress my tears. She was concerned and I made an excuse about a bad cold. But the corporal had just put me through a week of sleepless nights and absurd 'bull'. The abuse directed at me had mounted, leaving him annoyed in his warped way when I silently complied and refused to give up in front of him. I can only think of one other occasion when I cried. That was at the sale of Wally Hammond's mementos in Cheltenham. By then he had died, leaving little money, and his second wife and others were selling up. Everyone seemed to be moving around the lots with a guilty step. It was a truly poignant tableau of acrid reflections on a gifted life that drifted into virtual anonymity in South Africa. I had attended as a freelance journalist, working as it happened for the *Guardian*. When the sale was over – and some of the items had gone too cheaply – I walked back to my car and cried in my solitude. Does that make me a bad journalist?

Service life after Hereford came as a surge of relief. Most of us appeared spare to requirements and attended our pay parades with unease about what the RAF was going to find for us to do. With a ridiculous sense of misplacement it was even suggested, in a moment of madness, that I should try for a short-term commission. They needed no more than a nominal look at me to realise that I was definitely not officer material. But I was sent off for an Air Ministy interview which thankfully and sensibly was unproductive.

It took place on a Sunday morning on a day memorable for what happened on the Northern Line as I returned to my temporary base at Colindale. The one snatch of advice, given me in advance of my interview, was to read thoroughly one of the serious Sunday papers. I chose the *Observer* and went to the Air Ministry well briefed on the current international news. None of it came up; I daresay that the squadron leader who asked the questions had already made up his mind that I wasn't sartorially cut out for any Pilot Officer Foot role.

Soon I was heading back by tube in time for Sunday lunch at my station. During the journey I found myself sitting next to an attractive Indian lady in full sari regalia. She began a conversation which quickly moved on to Test cricket at her instigation. Had I ever been to a Test in India, she wondered? She had an impeccable accent and before long I was being given part of her life story, which hinted at a privileged domestic background, so much so that her father always invited the two teams to his residence whenever the Test was played locally.

We were the only two in the carriage and I was flattered that we were having such a pleasant chat about international cricket and famous players. She also declared that she liked my uniform, something that had never been said to me before. A pity the malicious corporal hadn't been an eavesdropper, I mused to myself. We got to Golders Green where rather formally we shook hands as she got up to leave. But first, to my utter surprise, she took my *Observer* and scribbled her name and the address of her London hotel on the front page. Then she was gone, as elegant as ever and with the deportment of a wealthy young woman no doubt creating a stir of admiration as she walked along the platform.

I left it for a week and then phoned the hotel. She was there, was pleased I had stayed in touch and yes, she would like tea at the Ritz. This was a somewhat grand gesture on my part but I felt she warranted that at least. It turned out she was on holiday in this country and was here for another fortnight or so. Over tea and cakes – which stretched my penny-pinching budget – I had the opportunity to study her features. She was probably ten years older than I was, undeniably good looking in a style that carried dignity and privilege. I did my best to exhume social graces and qualities that had mostly got lost amid the surfeit of obscenities and gobbled cookhouse pragmatism of Service life.

It must be said that she drastically misinterpreted my status. Over the next few days she suggested that we should go to a race meeting – I think it was Epsom though I can't remember for sure at this distance. She clearly didn't understand that RAF personnel at my level needed to be available for daily duty. Our pleasing, prim, educational liaison involved one visit of mine to the hotel where she was staying (she had caught chicken pox and was confined to bed). She quickly recovered and, with more hand shakes and a stolen, responsive kiss to hint at missed opportunities, she was gone. We had come from vastly different backgrounds and the irony was that she assumed I might be around regularly as her guide and social partner until she returned to India.

I was placed in various transit camps in the London area while the authorities were deciding what to do with me. Regularly I took the underground to the West End, to gaze in boyish excitement at the sheer purposeful bustle, the theatrical neon lights and Soho's furtive, seedier side streets.

For this I was prepared to moderate my criticism of National Service. It all seemed wonderfully sophisticated: the fleshy former actors I would recognise in the run-down pubs, their drinking funded now only by walk-on parts and the generosity of a fellow lush; oily foreigners who all looked like the brothel keepers I'd avidly read about; familiar names on shop fronts, pretty girls with vacuous eyes, men in a habitual hurry as they climbed stairways to clip-joint retreats for protection money reluctantly handed over.

On fiddled RAF shifts I went to the Windmill, not so much to see bare, shapely thighs as to hear comedians like Harry Secombe, Bruce Forsyth, Arthur English, Peter Sellers, then a chubby impressionist, Michael Bentine, Harry Worth and Tommy Cooper doing their best to convince the punters that it can be as much fun to laugh as to lech. Some of the comics, with their carefully devised scripts, were like unwelcome guests, ignored or unappreciated, agonising as they compromised their material.

The Windmill concept of continuous performances was bold and clever. There was an intimacy about the place with its touch of decadence that I found irresistible. I even wrote to the Windmill's musical director, asking if he would have a look at some of my lyrics, delicately attuned to what I saw as wholesome ambiguity.

Music hall hadn't yet gone for good. The fading ambience was much to my liking. Some of the speciality acts belonged more suitably to Continental circus. It often struck me that hastily hired musicians, brought in to bolster threadbare pit orchestras, were certainly not proficient at necessary sight-reading of the crumpled scores handed to them as they rushed at the last minutes into the theatre. But I would then see marvellous jugglers or, once at Fulham Broadway, a Jewish pianist who could play the classics and would then use an orange for all the black notes in his distinctive version of the *Warsaw Concerto*. The finest performers would obscure the repetitive boredom of the once excellent act that they had peddled round the country for years. They had the rare gift of making their decrepit jokes still sound new.

I must admit that for me those absolutely awful aspects of music hall, by then in some cases a ghastly symbol of inevitable cynicism, remained part of their antiquated charm. At the Queens, Poplar, where I had gone in exploration of London's East End entertainment, I was one of just eight in the audience. The principal comic came on for his first spot, told two or three jokes of Victorian vintage. He glared at his almost non-existent audience ... and walked off. He didn't come back for his publicised second appearance.

It was one of the most unprofessional things I ever saw on the British stage. There wasn't enough money at the box-office to give the eight of us our money back. I was appalled by what I had seen – and yet the comedian's torment continued to haunt me. What was he going through? How much of his own money had he lost on the week's show? Did he have the greater contempt for the few who watched, the jaded dancers who should have given up years before, the management's anger, or the comedian's own patronising valediction?

If this was National Service, I had to give it another chance. But I knew it was a brief bonus and was too good to last. At least two evenings a week I would go, in my uniform, and queue up at the Nuffield Centre, just across the road from Charing Cross Station. There were always theatre tickets to give away, not always to the best shows but still a creative gift to poorly paid servicemen. The Nuffield Centre was a popular meeting place for those of us who simply loved the theatre and didn't have the money to go. Apart from the free tickets, the building offered its own entertainment. It was used as a try-out venue for dozens of optimistic singers and comedians. The agents would come to watch, pull a face and leave early. But the few really vibrant acts were worth waiting for.

It was a sort of Discoveries Night, the artists lining up nervously for their names to be called. The singers had their music with them, handed hopefully to the resident pianist. What irritated me, and still does, was the number of comics whose unrelieved camp humour unbalanced their act. There had been so many transvestite revues during and after the war. Homosexual jokes are acceptable when delivered by gay performers. Too many had, with little additional imagination, capitalised on the success of Larry Grayson, Kenneth Williams and Frankie Howerd. There were too many imitators, too little originality. Camp comedy is not new. In the same way that so many of the earthy early 20th century women comedians were male impersonators, so talented pretty young men flogged with merciless repetition the easy subject of effeminacy. Comedians should be judged only on how funny they are, not exclusively by the disparity of gender.

About this time I read that National Servicemen had the chance, if they possessed any aptitude for languages, to apply for a place on the newly launched Joint Services School for Linguists (JSSL). The intention was to make them fluent in Russian, up to degree standard, in nine months. It was the time of the Cold War and in 1951 the scheme had in theory an aura of glamour. I immediately applied, pointing out that I had gained a credit in French in School Certificate. Almost by return I was informed that I'd been accepted and would be going to the School at Coulsdon, Surrey. Similar centres were set up at Bodmin and later Crail, in East Fife.

Rumours were rife and coloured as we fantasised about what might be involved. "Not so far off a bit of spying," an applicant with an Oxbridge bearing suggested. He wasn't so far from the truth. Months later it emerged that one of the course's graduates had been a Soviet spy, though the details of that Le Carré episode were never revealed in their tingling entirety.

The setting up of the languages school had clearly been an expensive operation. So the need for a successful academic return demanded a high standard of intense study. That didn't appear to bother the majority of the students. Many of them had come into the Services almost straight from school. The habit of absorbing knowledge – or Russian new words and grammar in this case – and the discipline of sitting exams were no obvious problem for them. I soon concluded, with apprehension, that I was surrounded by some of the country's brightest young intellectuals. The elite were whisked away for specialised tuition.

There were names later to be famous, who guaranteed a comparatively untaxing time for themselves as they learned Russian. I had no idea, for instance, that Alan Bennett, Michael Frayn and Dennis Potter were part of the select band of star language students. Sir Peter Hall and the controversial Cornish novelist DM Taylor were others. Many of them excelled. I didn't. I stayed the course for some months and, to my surprise, squeezed through various exams. But I'd left school several years before and the ability to retain a new alien and extended vocabulary now, while aiming at a passable version of basic Russian dialogue, was embarrassingly beyond me.

A small group of us, hardly renowned for linguistic prowess although we did our best, were convinced that the JSSL was based, as we saw it, on a monumental confidence trick. And we were the victims. Intelligence on the scope and methods of teaching us was significantly threadbare. The JSSL, still teasing our heads with Cold War imagery, was the Great Unknown.

We weren't told much in advance. But the general belief, accepted in naïve wonderment, was that we would be treated during the course in effect as civilians. We would miss all the nauseating excesses of 'bull' and would benefit from the relative comfort of 'undergraduate' tuition.

"We're on a great skive," one newly found mate assured me in intimate tones, "and we'll be officers in everything but name. No drill parades, no prats with two stripes belting out the orders. Plenty of weekend passes. And at the end a cushy time when we'll be pretending to be interpreters or monitoring signals from ships in the North Sea."

I didn't know from where he got all his information. But it put me in good heart as I collected a dozen school exercise books with the RAF crest on the front and awaited instructions.

Disillusion came in a matter of days. It was supposed to be a joint-service operation. To my horror, it was the army who supervised the drill and parade ground discipline. They had us out, in our heavy boots and distraught manners, before dawn. After that we piled into a succession of billets, taking our places behind one of the trestle tables. No time was wasted. On the first morning the teacher, with no pause for proper introductions, had us chanting everyday greetings and practising our goodnights in 'Janet and John' collective fashion.

Yes, the teachers: they created one of our greatest initial difficulties. They came in all sizes and dialects. We can only assume that the manner of their recruitment, and crash course on how to handle bright, frustrated teenagers, gave the JSSL principals considerable stress and far more than growing pains. We did our best to wrap our tongues around rugged Eastern European consonants. We familiarised ourselves with additional letters from the alphabet we'd not seen in print before. So it went on every day – army drill without too much compassion (though still not half as bad as Hereford) and study in a cold billet where the windows rattled in the wind or the drab room was filled with smoke from the coke stoves which in turn we dutifully stoked.

The tutors, an unsmiling lot with grey faces and a presence as self-conscious as ours, struggled to find a rapport. For us, the constant strain was in understanding what they wanted, indeed needed, to impart. They came from many sources – their voices demanded our unwavering attention. "They could do with a course in linguistics more than we do," was a regular despairing dig from the classes. Such ironies were part of a National Serviceman's life.

We had one or two students with a bent towards cartoonist traits. They took a timely break from our choral 'Janet and John' with illustrations of our teachers. The sheer ethnic range had a compelling, if icy, feel. There were the White Russian émigrés, strutting out of the classroom at the end of the session with an aristocratic grandeur that had never been wholly cast aside during their historic plight. Then there were the contrasting defectors from the barely known terrain of Europe's eastern borders. That was Coulsdon; it is unlikely that Bodmin and Crail were that much better.

But I know that for some students it was a stimulating time. The outstanding ones were filched for specialist roles and really were treated as civilians. For them it was a well-spent two years. By 1960 the bold, experimental, head-aching course had come to an end. It is hard to tell how many of those raw servicemen went on professionally to benefit. Indeed, how much did the country?

I envied the high-fliers and their facility for foreign language. By the end of five or six months, however, I'd had enough. With a sheepish feeling of failure, I asked to be taken off the course. I knew that I would miss international athlete Gordon Pirie's training runs around Coulsdon and Caterham; I would miss the generosity of fellow student John Mills, so proud of his racer bike and yet prepared to let me borrow it to ride into the West End for a Saturday night play. I would miss the metamorphosis of one particular student, en route to Keble College and a career as a clergyman. His normal demeanour in the day time carried the gentle, spiritual qualities of his future calling. But once or twice he woke the billet with the obscene shouts of a young man in torment. "I'll fill in the whole fucking lot of you," he screamed. The rest of the billet sat up in bed to listen to his monologue of compelling hate. We never mentioned it to him next morning. I must leave a shrink to work it out. What we did hope was that his threat was limited to the instructors and not the whole of the God-fearing human race.

For the rest of my time in National Service I was stationed at Thorney Island, near Portsmouth, where I climbed marginally the pay structure as a leading aircraftsman. Part of my time was spent plotting navigation hazards and distributing pre-flight chocolate to trainee aircrew. My days in the confectioners' trade demanded infinite honesty. So I was mortified to be hauled out of my bed by the RAF police one morning after being on all-night shift, and accused of stealing chocolates. I accompanied the Service police officer to my flight lieutenant's office and was questioned unpleasantly for half an hour.

It was a cruel, unfounded accusation levelled against someone who has never been guilty of the theft of a penny-piece in his life. In fact, the chocolates were eventually found in another cupboard. My RAF officer failed to offer even a token apology as I was sent back to complete my broken night's sleep.

I liked Thorney Island. On free nights I went into Portsmouth, often missing the last train back. It was a bonus that I could doss at a Services Club just over the road from the railway station. It cost half a crown, was warm and afforded a hard though welcome pillow as I folded my coat and placed it on the rusty radiator. I slept, more or less, in a sitting position. Demob was approaching, time to renew old journalistic friendships and swap stories of National Service traumas. Girl friends were becoming a serious consideration as the loins began to ache. I went to dance classes at Chichester and hitched a lift back as pillion rider with a young navigation trainee officer. From Chichester railway station I went courting, as we called it, on Goodwood racecourse. If Pompey were at home, I would go to watch them at Fratton Park's functional enclosure. When RAF Thorney Island started a magazine, I was asked for a feature. My choice was Phyllis Dixey, topping the bill at the Theatre Royal. She was the most demure of strippers, a teasing, suggestive, graceful one-time ballet dancer who always promised, in that nicely modulated voice, rather more than she personally delivered. Hers were the quiet, seductive sentences rather than too much expanse of flesh. But Jack Tracey, her husband and manager, hovered during the whole of the interview as if not really approving of her intimate thoughts being conveyed in a small-circulation Services magazine.

She was still a modest coup for us. The peek-a-boo girl wasn't at all a bad way to sign off my time-wasting National Service.

8

A PROPER JOURNALIST

My first working day in Bristol was memorable, not for any introductory by-lines, more for the acquiring of new routines in an unfamiliar newsroom, where the reporters, all looking terribly sophisticated, cheery and knowledgeable, sat round a large table, laden with old newspapers, grimy notebooks with no blank pages, and bent spikes that eloquently conveyed the fate of rejected stories and superfluous council minutes.

Reg Eason, the news editor, addressed his staff with a polite if deceptive "Mr" or "Miss" prefix. "Ah, Mr Foot, our newcomer. This is when we go through all the other papers, looking for follow-ups. And I've got one for you straightaway. There's a marathon pianist, playing non-stop from a hall in Old Market. The *Western Daily Press* haven't given her much of a show, although it appears she's heading for a record. Perhaps you can look in and see her."

I studied her picture as the morning paper was passed to me. She was hardly glamorous – or young.

The news editor was as ever assertive and in a hurry. He decided to test me out. "Tell me, Mr Foot, what are you going to ask her?" That was a tricky one, not something I'd been specifically trained to answer in my untaxing Yeovil days. Inspiration came, however. "As she's been playing for nearly a week without getting off the stool, I think I'd want to know about her personal hygiene."

That caused an instant stir of communal interest and amusement. Reg may have wondered what sort of reporter he'd taken on from rural Somerset. The voluptuous June, her desk strategically placed by the news editor to give him viewing rights of her undulating frontage, said aloud that she thought it was a valid question. Meanwhile I was sent off to interview the tired-eyed pianist, whose repertoire was boringly basic. There were no other spectators to pay their shilling while I watched and chatted intermittently with her.

Yes, she played the classics as well as Eve Boswell. Yes, she did pop out to the lavatory "although I'd rather you didn't mention that". Yes, she did once go nearly ten days without a proper break. Yes, she did have a nap in the middle of the night, if there was no-one around. I wasn't wholly convinced about her claims of being a marathon pianist – or her ability to give us a genuine snatch of Beethoven. It could be that I did her a disservice.

By the time I arrived back in the office, Reggie had lost interest in any supposed newsworthiness for the pianist. There was a suspected murder picked up on the morning police calls. "Just two or three paragraphs on this woman at the most. Take them into the sub-editors and give me a black."

I had put on a suit for my first day. The news editor gave me a full-length inspection and seemed to approve of my appearance if not my theoretical line of questioning. But the newsroom was a frantically busy one. The typewriters rattled in clumsy though efficient hands. The phones, scattered around the untidy table, kept ringing as we in turn grabbed the nearest like the neurotic hand-bell ringers back in St Michael's belfry.

"And one other thing, Mr Foot. You're not working for the *Western Gazette* any longer. Short sentences, don't waste words. You are writing for passengers on the bus."

I had not yet found any accommodation so had booked myself into the YMCA, just round the corner from my office, for a few nights. They directed me to the overflow annexe, which happened to be an erstwhile women's reformatory. It was constructed like one. The aura of authority still persisted; so did the smell of cheap disinfectant.

My spectrum of unlikely first-day experiences, professional and human, was not yet over. I went searching for a nearby café late that night and found one still serving modest, greasy suppers. It was populated by half a dozen women with pale, unhealthy complexions and language guaranteed to extend my vocabulary of enforced expletives. I soon realised it was where the prostitutes came when their back-seat-in-the-car work was done.

That night they were in an ugly mood. Their voices were raised and some of them began to fight. A glass door was smashed and before long half a dozen police officers arrived. I remained mesmerised. This was Bristol at its most seedy, and I was determined not to move. Several of the women, their thick lips smeared with the remnants of crudely applied lipstick, appeared to be into their sixties. They continued to hire out their arid bodies because it was the only trade they knew. The arguing continued, and some of the offenders were unceremoniously carted off to the station.

I went back to my cramped bed and wrote it up. Not too long … short sentences … just right to read on the bus on the way into work. I would never have dared to turn it into a news story for the *Gazette*. But I was given a frisson of pride to discover that the *World* had used it on page three with a two-column intro GIRLS EJECTED AFTER CITY CAFÉ INCIDENT. All my own work. I was in business.

For some weeks the stories that came my way were devoid of similar drama. Maybe I was patronising the wrong late-night caffs. By now I had been transferred to the YMCA proper where I could buy meals on the premises and, as long as I kept out of the path of the disconcerting number of homosexuals who roamed the upstairs corridors when the rest of us were in bed, life was stimulating and uncomplicated.

In the middle of one night there was a knock on my door. I hesitated, aware of the prowlers, before opening it. John Bennett, the paper's film critic and assistant editor, was there. He'd just returned from a cinema premiere and was in a state of some anxiety. He blurted out that there had been serious floods in Weymouth overnight, that caravans had been washed away and lives were in danger.

Weymouth was marginally in our circulation area. This was, however, a big story and we needed to be there. John had checked the emergency list of reporters and saw that I lodged nearest to the office and the office car. He said he had arranged with the night-watchman to open up the garage. "You do drive, don't you?" he asked as an after-thought.

I dressed in a frenzy of expectation. So far I had never been entrusted with the office Ford Pop. So I'd be learning – and thinking – on the job. I stuffed a virgin notebook into my pocket and made sure I had enough coppers for the phone calls I knew I would have to make. I was familiar with Weymouth from all the annual choir and Sunday School outings I once used to make. The journey there, though, was a blur. Too many premature angles were already scurrying around in my head.

The floods were as bad as John Bennett had warned. My basic newspaper training came to my aid, and I stopped at Weymouth's police station for the duty sergeant and his augmented staff to tell me what exactly was happening. Frank, an experienced reporter from the *Daily Express*, was already there. He sensed I was a young lad not too sure how to tackle my assignment. "Leave your car here and come along with me," he said. That kind of generous spirit was something I recurrently met and valued. I'm not at all sure that it still exists in the reportage world of laptops and impersonal facades of token communication out on the stories as eager agency journalists need ruthlessly to compete with a declining number of staff men.

As usual there were conflicting reports of the flood damage. But by 7.30 a.m. I had enough for my first piece. It ran to more than fifteen hundred words. There was no time for any fancy descriptive phrases, although alliterative images like "raging rivers" slipped in. I wrote of ruined holidays and chalets floating past like so much match-wood. I quoted the Chief Constable and members of the council and some of the victims I had already seen in the pre-dawn confusion.

Back in the *World* office, my lengthy first-edition copy was running late with no more than a hurried transfer-charge call and message from me that it would soon be on the way. Reg, the news editor, was apoplectic as he swore to no-one in particular: "Where the bloody hell is his copy? Does he even know our edition times? Why did we get him out of bed? He's probably never covered a big story before. When it comes, we'll probably have to rewrite the whole lot. Christ, what a disaster!"

Even as he blasphemed, I was on the phone dictating, partly from my notes, partly off the cuff. It was the first really big story with which I'd ever been entrusted And it was OK. Even from the pavements of Weymouth, running with floodwater as they still were, I imagined I could hear Reg and the room full of subs sighing in unison with relief. My report was spread over the front page and two pages inside. I wrote of the rescue work that had already begun and of holiday plans in ruins. I wrote of 600 homeless people. (It was a justifiably hazardous statistic I had heard mentioned. There was no chance yet to verify it.) It helped that by accident I also found a family from Bristol, bedraggled and miserable. The human interest, lifeblood of popular journalism, wasn't ignored.

The *World* seemed pleased apparently with the mature way I handled the floods. I visited the holiday caravan sites and the river banks that had burst. I latched on, privately triumphant, to every distressed family with an address in or near to Bristol. I motored to Bowleaze and Lulworth Coves.

"You gave us a scare but it all worked out well. Think we'll leave you down there for a day or two. Let's see, don't you come from near Weymouth?"

"Well, 25 miles away at least. But happy to stay with the story, Mr Eason."

The *World*, desperate of necessity to look after their pennies, suggested I should stay with my parents. I was proud of my proper newspaperman's status and willingly agreed. Some of the fellow reporters were altogether more pointed. "That's the one trouble with our paper – it's run by mean sods. You should have been put up in a Dorset hotel." I was in no mood to complain. The scope of the story meant more to me than where I was going to sleep.

Yet compensations weren't hard to find. Most of us in the office were about the same age. We went to each other's parties, had coffee at Carwardine's as we waited for the jury to come back. Norman, the office drunk, always wore a formal dark grey suit. He was the industrial and trades union correspondent. Most social evenings he could be relied on for his bizarre impersonation of a Mother Superior, though we were none too certain of his Catholic roots. Norman, who spoke with an appropriate clerical voice, was apt to pounce with enthusiasm on new male members of staff. He saw them as long-term drinking companions and that no doubt accounts for the solicitous way he showed concern for my well-being during my initial months at Northcliffe House. He twice took me out in the office car, unofficially commandeered, for interminable sessions at the pubs he knew intimately for their landlords' after-hours proclivities. It was impossible to escape and I would arrive back furtively at the austere YMCA premises in time for breakfast

The YMCA was locked up for the night at an ungodly hour, so I'd had to walk Bristol's central streets for a couple of hours. It was on one such night that I met Tom Walker, a truly remarkable vagabond-philosopher. He had a splendid white beard and an accent that suggested he had seen better days. Tom was 80 and was walking, in his own unscheduled time, from Exeter back to his old people's home at Rutland. I decided on the spot to write about him. An empathetic sub-editor headed it ARISTOCRAT OF TRAMPS. Once Tom had been the political agent for Sir Alfred Yeo, the Liberal MP for South Poplar. He authenticated the claim by pulling out a pile of faded pictures and newspaper cuttings from his brown paper carrier bag. There was no mistaking the identity. I noticed the cross round his neck. "Religious, are you?" I asked. He chuckled. "I suppose you could call me more a Roaming Catholic."

He was clearly hungry but I could think of nowhere that was open apart from Temple Meads Station. By now we'd built up an unlikely relationship for four o'clock in the morning. I cherished the conversation, all about that self-induced freedom from rigid convention, and I impetuously stopped a taxi. At the railway station, I remember, they would not allow old Tom and his brown paper bag onto the platform. So I carried him out a cup of tea and a bun. His manners were impeccable as we shook hands.

There were dozens of chance interviews like this. If Mr Eason wondered what I was doing around the almost deserted streets of Bristol in the early hours, he never asked. The *World* used the majority of my stories, covering most of the human scene. I'm not too sure what the news editor made of me. His remarks to me were inclined to carry an element of asperity. But I liked his news sense and the urgency that he imparted. After my somnolent days at the *Gazette*, they were attributes I badly needed.

I was married six months after moving to Bristol. Anne tolerated my irregular hours. She was at times caught up in my journalistic enthusiasm, quickly learning the slang language of my trade. Court reporting was a particular joy to me. If I was lucky enough to be covering a murder trial and the verdict was imminent, I would phone Anne and tell her to leave the ironing and come to the court's public gallery instead. When I was reporting on a county cricket match being played at one of the outgrounds with limited press facilities, Anne would come with me. She knew I was in competition with the *Evening Post*'s excellent, news-conscious Peter Godsiff and that I needed to send regular updates for the various editions. We would recce the surrounds to the ground before the start of play, to find a phone box within reasonable walking distance. In the summers when we had a small son in a pushchair, my wife would loyally walk backwards and forwards, phoning my revised copy. As a family we didn't much approve of dummies but Anne needed on occasions to keep our son quiet as the latest batch of purple prose was being sent back to the copy-takers in Colston Avenue.

Cricket and sunshine were all very well. George Brown, MP and notorious boozer, was a different prospect. He had come to Bristol's Grand Hotel to speak at a literary dinner and I was given two tickets to report the event. Anne and I were seated at a table next to the one where the Foreign Secretary was drinking far more than he was eating. His high decibel level never lessened as the courses were rotated. Then it was his turn to address the large gathering of black-tie book readers and their ladies.

George Brown was unsteady as he got up. And then for a reason that still eludes me – maybe it was because we were within convenient eye range – he zoomed in on Anne and me. "Well, I can see what kind of company this is. It's what is wrong with society. You two … yes, you. I don't know who you are. But I can see what you're like … Cosy Bristol suburbia. Big house … no doubt three cars in the drive … Clifton toffs … And don't look away when I'm talking to you …" And on he went, stumbling over his words, forgetting what he wanted to say, obsessed with class divisions.

He sat down to muted applause. No-one was quite sure what he intended to offer his audience. As for three cars in the drive, if only. We couldn't afford yet to run one; and we still had the orange box, now painted it was true, that served as our bookcase and point of reference.

Drunken politicians aren't of course unknown to journalists. Some are sober, polite and personable. Michael Foot waffled but we got on well with him because professionally he was one of us and was a nice man, happiest of all in the Home Park grandstand. Tony Benn had decent qualities, though he never quite acquired the working-class psyche he professed to know so well. He also made us uncomfortable as he insisted on bringing out his own cassette to record us recording him. The trouble with Margaret Thatcher and Ted Heath was that they lacked humanity.

Harold Macmillan, whom I interviewed several times, was at heart an actor and could be most engaging. I was once sent to his hotel room to do a radio interview just before he was due to address several hundred doting supporters. He was in ill health and he asked me to take his arm as we came down in the lift. He was so pallid and shaky that I feared I might have a fatality on my hands. We got to the doorway of the ballroom where he was due to make his speech and the cheering began. I looked at him and suddenly saw his face light up. He was loved by his audience; even at his age he was in spirit more matinée idol than politician. Parody wasn't so far away behind that familiar moustache.

As an evening paper journalist, less shy than I used to be, I particularly enjoyed the sheer variety of my work. Versatility was necessary. So was the skill of listening. I had rapidly realised that a modestly educated reporter like me couldn't possibly have a working knowledge of so many subjects. But it seemed patently rude and naïve to reveal one's ignorance to the specialist we were about to question. The case for a little bluff, backed up by timely snatches of research, is surely obligatory, not to be readily condemned.

I liked writing on a wide range of topics. Asked once to produce at short notice a feature for a *Financial Times* supplement, my piece of alien journalism must have pleased them enough to lead to up to a dozen follow-ups. They were, I like to think, well written and posed the right questions about high finance in the regional, national and even global level. It must have gone to my head. I wrote to the *Sunday Times* Atticus column, implying that I could conjure up regular, exclusive pieces from the West Country. Hunter Davies must have been doing the column at the time. "Send me some jokes instead," was his kindly, if slightly pejorative reply.

About this time my excessive attempts at diversification led to an unexpected invitation to do some pop and jazz reviews for *Melody Maker*. Jazz I liked as a non-specialist. Pop, much of which to me lacked tunefulness, lyrics, decent singers and some hint of originality, only suggested my unsuitability to offer a judgement. I covered concerts fronted, for instance, by Duke Ellington, Count Basie, Stan Kenton, Woody Herman and many of the other legendary jazz figures. They were a joy I hadn't imagined would come my way.

My *MM* commissions continued and I had every reason to thank a National Service friend who worked in Tin Pan Alley and who provided a number of features. I was, however, a trifle fearful when asked to do a lengthy interview with Buddy Rich, the celebrated drummer. "He's a difficult customer – you'll do well to get him to see you." My problem was that the magazine wanted a technical article about drumming. As arranged I waited with some trepidation in the lounge of the Grand Hotel for Buddy Rich to return after his concert at Bristol's Colston Hall. At 11 p.m. he arrived; at 3.30 a.m. we were still there. He spoke in language I could understand, going to infinite pains to explain the intimacies of playing his own frenetic style of personalised percussion at the highest of levels. The early words of warning from others were utterly misplaced. We drank whisky and he talked. It was just what the *Melody Maker* wanted.

My briefly exaggerated reputation as this wide-ranging music reviewer led to a visit to Yeovil Liberal Hall, a building once well known to me in my greenhorn days when the reporters went there to play cards on Saturday mornings. "We'd like you to have a look at this lot. Don't know too much about them. They're apparently called The Who."

Professionalism hadn't yet caught up with them. They arrived late, grumpy and disorganised. As for their playing, it was less riveting than their manic antics and instrument disintegration. They pranced round the stage, treating their guitars as if they were unbridled wild animals intent on destruction. The sound level was as suspect as the band's knowledge of the running order and collective discipline.

I left with a throbbing headache – and two questions for me to work out. Would this scruffy group ever get anywhere, smashing up the furniture like that? And what was that rather pleasant smell?

My grandiose reports continued to satisfy the *MM*'s affable news editor, Jerry Dawson, allowing him to substantiate previously depleted coverage of the music scene in the West Country. I wrote the apposite phrases with increasing confidence. Soon I was asked to listen to and review Jethro Tull – and Otis Redding who with pleasant and unusual modesty said they were a fine audience in Bristol but didn't hear him at his best. Sounded pretty good to me. I remember him adding: "When I go to a recording studio, you know, I make up the words as I go along." That explained a lot.

By way of an unexpected journalistic bonus, the magazine gave me a page lead when Dizzy Gillespie appeared at the Colston Hall. The temperamental musician got engrossingly involved in a row with sections of the audience. It lasted for ten minutes, as abuse was noisily traded. Gillespie's insults, some of them inarticulate, were matched by those of jazz lovers who argued that they had been short-changed. "The audience was the worst I ever played to. Let's get out of this place." That at least is the sanitised version of Dizzy's exit. Some of the audience walked out. Meanwhile, I retrieved my grubby notebook from a back pocket (I never believed in too many cumbersome, overloaded notebooks, maybe because my shorthand was as unreliable as in those greenhorn days when I shared my Pitman scribbles with the blousey tutor's sprawling feline companions).

It was an occasion of confusion but no more than when I took my first steps as a football reporter covering Bristol City. I'd been showing some aptitude, it appears, in assisting the sports desk with football and cricket at a lower level. Now the City man had gone from the *World* and there was a vacancy for me. What appealed, after the years of objective reporting, was the opportunity to be able to express an opinion in print. I didn't have simply to regurgitate the platitudes of the local Member of Parliament as he lectured blandly to the transfixed faithful. I could actually say if the centre forward had a stinker.

My first game at Ashton Gate was against Liverpool, then in the second division. I hadn't met any of the Bristol players and the only Liverpool one I would have recognised was the wonderful Billy Liddell whose picture I had previously cut out and put in my scrapbook. In addition I knew from my cigarette cards that the visitors played in red shirts – although I had forgotten that, because of a clash of colours, they'd have to change their strips for this visit to the West Country

It was the days of the *Pink Un* and the *Green Un*. I was confronted, on my debut, with 2,000 words of crisp commentary dictated straight into my phone. Nothing except perhaps the goal-scorers was written down. It struck me as a challenging exercise and I was up for it. That was until 20 minutes into the game when I recognised Billy Liddell – in a white shirt. And wasn't that tall, strong player at the other end of the field John Atyeo? In red?

In panic I realised I had been describing all the wrong players – and wrong teams – for 20 minutes. I sank deep into my hard Ashton Gate seat and evaluated my options. Dare I tell George Baker, my affable sports editor, what calamitous, inaccurate commentary I had offered our readers, and would I be now worth keeping on the staff? Or should I just pretend that everything was fine, hoping that no-one would notice? Perspiring freely, I opted for bluff. My duplicitous decision succeeded, and there wasn't a single complaint. What conclusion do we draw from readers' powers of concentration?

The *Pink Un* was on the street less than half an hour after the final whistle. I marvelled many times over the proficiency of the system, inevitable literals excused. In those early exchanges with Liverpool, no-one had scored. City went on to win, so who was going to berate me for that burst of emergency fiction? No-one blissfully had even noticed.

9

DRINKS WITH RACHEL ROBERTS

In the same way as many shy lads, I liked performing. The measure of anonymity, as I obscured my own tentative personality and took on another one, was something I found appealing. Before I got to grammar school I was writing scripts and appearing in village shows of unmitigated enthusiasm and dubious artistic value.

East Coker Boys and Girls Club's annual variety show played to packed houses. The improvised stage on trestle tables creaked precariously and the faded turquoise curtains were badly torn. But such minor flaws were ignored. Don, the headmaster's son, painted the scenery. We recruited a senior pianist who helped with the haphazard business of producing our varied and at times over-ambitious programme. We leaned on a soprano, the wife of the pianist, for a spot in each half, to invest our three-evening cavalcade with a touch of class. There were also a lightning artist from the village, and two young accordionists who did gimmicky much-enjoyed things as they played each other's musical instruments.

The East Coker show

From the age of 14, inspired by what I had heard on the wireless, I was trying my hand at stand-up comedy. That was surely a physical misnomer. I did my eight-minute act from a sitting-down posture. For some inexplicable reason, I performed in my pyjamas and with my bare feet in a bowl of water. It guaranteed an early obligatory laugh and I think it was again linked to my need for anonymity as I assumed a distracting persona.

I wasn't nervous. My script was relatively original and localised. In those slightly show-off days, I had a cheeky talent for working an audience. I still remember a night when a small party from the village of Nether Compton had surprisingly come to watch. "You all know Nether Compton," I told the bulging crowd of eighty or so. "The brother of Denis Compton." They liked our youthful corn.

I doubled-up as a pretty dreadful impressionist, though I did decent impersonations of John Arlott and Ralph Wightman, a popular broadcaster with a strong West Country burr. I used to close by announcing that I would humbly and patriotically like to give them Winston Churchill's famous wartime address. The audience would go very quiet while deliberately I took a long cigar from my pocket as I got to my feet.

Suddenly, from one of the front rows, a triumphant voice shouted out. "Ten, Downing Street!" It had come from George Mullard, the vicar, and he'd ruined my best gag.

That was bad enough. But he later complained at what he saw as bad taste and too much sexual content in one of our sketches. "Watch it in future," he intoned. And I'd always thought he was broad-minded.

Our shows, enjoyed by our relatives, were mostly a success. Don, who wrote the majority of the sketches with me, also practised unceasingly until he could master a basic Fred Astaire routine with cane and tap dance steps. On reflection, there was far too much plagiarism in our playlets but litigation didn't occur to us. There was one classic Bobby Howes sketch which we dared to perform. It featured a nymphomaniac lady of means (played by a boy with a penchant for decorous transvestism) and her compliant butler. Sophisticated and saucy stuff from the Boys' Club.

My affection for the theatre persisted. I must have admitted it to Mr Eason. To my dismay I soon found myself covering dozens of amateur productions. There were some outstanding ones in Bristol and rather a lot of appalling ones. An obvious shortcoming of amateurs is that too often they seem incapable of taking a non-incestuous look at their portfolio of plays, performances and musicals. Their principals uncritically imagine they are performing in the West End. Off stage, they are inclined to bicker too much and disapprove of how the auditions went. Often the contentious thespian politics on rehearsal nights are infinitely more riveting than the sum total of drama as the plots unfold.

I used to produce a weekly column for the amateur stage. Harassed producers would confide in me. There seemed to be a surfeit of flirting within the company and marriages, affected in some cases by the pseudo-romantic dialogue and sexy nuances on stage, collapsed permanently.

Anne and I attended church halls in most of Bristol's suburban outposts. We travelled on the bus. In the middle of winter we were sometimes so cold that we deliberately rode an extra stop or two on the way home. It wasn't an aspect of journalism much to my liking. But I tried to review the plays with a measure of kindly encouragement. I'd knock out my half a dozen paragraphs in front of the one-bar electric fire as my young wife poached an egg for us. And there were other bonuses.

An actor, Henry Woolf, who had been round for supper and to discuss the work of the recently emerged Bristol University drama department, had asked me to look in and see a new play, completed by a chum of his in 48 hours. Henry was the producer. The play had been written, I was told, by a struggling repertory actor from Bournemouth. Inside five minutes I was entrapped by the spare word patterns and the gripping atmosphere he had created. Here was an unscheduled dramatic treat. The 26-year-old author meant nothing to me but I wrote: "This writer must go on writing. I'm so glad I didn't miss his unusual play." I do hope that instant judgement doesn't at this distance sound mildly pompous.

The play was *The Room* and the author was Harold Pinter. I was told later that it was the first time one of his plays had been reviewed.

Years after I received a letter from Pinter. He had read a cricket book of mine, based on the gifted and finally tragic life of Somerset's Harold Gimblett. He had, as a cricketing addict, liked the book and saw its potential as a stage play. "What about a one-man character study? The biography, which ends in suicide, has all the strands of a powerful play."

It was marvellously flattering. He said he was too busy at the moment to pursue the idea but, if I shared his enthusiasm, he would come back to me. He never did. John Cleese was another to see stage possibilities in the sad life and death of Test cricketer Gimblett.

Gimblett was someone I knew quite well and who wanted me to put his words and opinions on paper. It was an amiable, if eventually depressing, relationship. Harold topped himself before the book was published; his wife, Rita, kept herself doggedly alive and then died on the day of publication. John Cleese was as eager as Pinter had been. He said he was coming down to Weston-super-Mare for the cricket festival and might it be possible to have a professional chat. By now, my private excitement as a relatively unworldly reporter was understandably growing.

We met at Clarence Park in the tea interval. Autograph seekers had spotted him and were making life intolerable for him. He released choice words and in a flash of manic temperament not too removed from the *Fawlty Towers* maelstrom, took his famous long, spindly legs off the heightened wooden seat, enough for me hesitantly to introduce myself.

"Ah yes, we've things to discuss. Come to the Grand Atlantic this evening for a drink. Half past eight. We can't talk with all this hubbub."

He had calmed down by then and called in on the way to the hotel to see his mother, who was staying in a local residential home. Clearly sharing my own affection for Somerset cricket and the wondrous batting of Gimblett – at least on one of the ex-cricketer's good days – Cleese pondered the various directions that a stage drama like this one could be explored and written. I got the firm impression that he warmed increasingly to being involved himself in a play about the county's 'tormented genius'. We talked for a long time, or rather John Cleese did most of the talking. He, like Pinter, was too busy at the moment to tackle the project. But he thought he would be back to me. The world of dramatic writing is caught up, alas. in a thousand spurts of transitory effervescence. For so many reasons, good ideas get discarded. The life and death of Harold Gimblett never quite made it beyond the stage of spinning round in the actor's fertile head.

At the *World* I progressed to the role of principal drama critic. I now covered all the plays at the Bristol Old Vic, touring shows at the Hippodrome and in Bath. The responsibility bothered me at times. Plagiarised sketches and a bit of jolly ad-lib when the turquoise curtains got stuck at East Coker were all very well. *Hamlet* and *Lear* were something else. They presented a new intellectual challenge, quite apart from demanding a necessary familiarity with the text on my part. I had read somewhere that the true duty of a critic should be to go to the production with no pre-conceived opinions or prejudices, but to be an uncluttered representative of ordinary people sitting to the left and right of him in the theatre. That appeared to me to be sound advice. I should go, I told myself, without any semblance of affectation. If I didn't like the play, I should say so in simple English, leaving pretentious and flowery verdicts to others in the audience who in any case stifled me with those well-rehearsed first night monologues of grandiloquent scholarship as they sipped their gin and tonics.

It wasn't always easy for me. I found at times I was more comfortable assessing a modern play than a classical tragedy. Anne came with me although on principle we never discussed the production until I'd written my piece. An added hazard for me was the lack of time in composing it.

By now I was working virtually full-time on the sports staff. Somehow I had to dovetail my overnight Ashton Gate football preview article or promised interview with a Gloucestershire bowler on a hat-trick, with the latest first night of wordy brilliance in cobbled King Street.

The patience of the accommodating George Baker, who happened fortunately to like going to the theatre himself, must have been sorely tested. I can't remember him swearing – such a rarity for a newspaper journalist – but he surely did under his breath as I struggled to complete and hand in my review, when clashing wretchedly, at 8 o'clock in the morning, with the sports back-page lead urgently needed for the first edition. It wasn't just the strain of writing in confusing duplicate. I chronically lacked elbow-room, too. The *World*, a victim of the vicious newspaper war which once raged through the provinces, with Northcliffe ironically brash and buoyant, was now in decline. The pages were fewer, the typographical errors more plentiful. The good writers stayed but their interest was by now more romantic than realistic. They blanched at the stories, many of them true, of how the newsagents were told to sell only the *Post*s, keeping the successive supplies of latest-edition *World*s out of sight. And yet, significantly, *Post* reporters would share a beer with us and admit they'd prefer to work for us. Ours remained, it was claimed, a happier paper. The trouble was that we were being made to suffer for the manner, full of arrogance and commercial largesse, that had characterised the Northcliffe-Rothermere arrival in the late 1920s – followed by the adroit way the *Post* in turn fought back, supported by a clever, psychological wave of local sentiment and even sanctimonious, misplaced rallying calls from a bishop's pulpit.

But the *World*'s soaring heights of circulation and pre-eminence had now gone. The balance of shares changed the face of Bristol newspapers. That prominent building of ours in central Colston Avenue, once choked with the presence of bustling newspaper vans, was still there. More and more of its offices, however, were having to be hired out. And that was where, in a confined, frustrated space, we did our best to work. The sports staff of five squeezed around a shabby piece of furniture no bigger than a card table. We shared it with our books of reference, dictionaries and those omni-present spikes.

I am not a militant by nature. But one afternoon, as against the odds I sub-edited a stack of hand-written skittles results from Bridgwater, I become so exasperated by the conditions that, somewhat melodramatically, I placed my chair on the table – and loftily sat on it there for the rest of the afternoon. I feared that the table might collapse, but it defiantly held firm, just as my protest did. My drastic furniture readjustment caused a stir and led to a silently eloquent inspection by the editor. By next morning, another chair and tatty filing cabinet had been added to the sports staff inventory.

Reg Eason must have felt he continued to have claims on me. "Mr Foot (the form of address remained as formal as ever), did I hear that you were due to have a day off at the end of the week?" What, I asked myself, was coming? "Do you think you can possibly do a story for me?"

He never gave time for a reasoned interruption. "It's all this trouble at the Theatre Royal. We really must carry something. You know, 'The Queen and the Rebels'. The *Post* are beginning to sniff that it's turning into a big one."

It was a powerful political play by Ugo Betti and the mild-mannered Bristol Old Vic director, John Moody, may well have opted for a little mischief when he included it in the current programme of plays. Not that he could possible have foreseen the extent of middle-class outrage that followed the opening night. Dozens walked out. Letters to the papers – ours and the opposition's – were multiplying. One extremist among the irate correspondents said that the theatre, the oldest working playhouse in the country, should be closed. The text and treatment were certainly robust for the time. The action touched on sadism and what some saw as sexual perversion. But it was also an articulate commentary on uglier aspects of society around the world. I hadn't got too perplexed by the play I had seen. Yet the public's reaction was unabated. "It's a revolting play, so unrestrained in its bestiality that it makes you wonder how an audience can be expected to sit through it," thundered one typical letter.

Mr Moody did his best to placate his body of long-standing Bristol Old Vic reactionaries. "Ugo Betti is a former High Court judge," as if that meant too much. I looked up my notes the other day, to discover that the company director had been forced to say that Betti was a very religious man. "The theme of all his plays is the nobility of the humblest of humans under stress because of the terrible conditions in the world." Religious or not, the cascading storm of protest was unprecedented in the history of Bristol's famous and illustrious theatre.

"So can I rely on a strong feature from you?"

I looked at Mr Eason, knowing that my intended day off was superseded and that there would need to be explanations to offer my wife. "You'd like me to see John Moody?"

"I think you should go straight to Rachel Roberts, who is the company's leading actress after all. Take her out to lunch."

That, I could only assume, was a joke. We didn't take actresses out for a meal because we couldn't afford to. Our lunch allowance on a special assignment was half a crown, and that made no concessions towards the guest. But Miss Roberts wasn't in the next play and was not in rehearsal. Slightly apprehensively, I phoned her at the stage door and she agreed to see me the following day at the actors' favourite pub, The Old Duke, just across the road from the Vic.

I had not met Rachel Roberts before, although I was aware that she had a thirst and, despite past restraints by having a Baptist minister as a father, was renowned for her salty line in dialogue. She was married to actor Alan Dobie and had, of course, not yet professionally progressed to film parts or a glamorous marriage to Rex Harrison

Her first request, before we got into the bar, was for a large martini. For the next three hours she was congenial company. She didn't offer me a drink, though why should she have? She was in loud, anecdotal and often indiscreet mood. The accent became more Welsh as her glass was replenished. I assumed she was going to be a star one day and encouraged her to go on talking At one point, to my fiscal embarrassment, I ran out of money, managing fortuitously to borrow some more from a rat-catcher friend of mine who was in the bar on good terms with most of the actors, not least because he acted as an alarm clock for them. He roused them for morning rehearsal after they had dossed down on communal mattresses in a fellow thespian's untidy flat.

Rachel Roberts gave me a memorably raw performance in that King Street pub, enough for the colourful profile that the news editor demanded. I'm not too sure what her non-Conformist family made of her desperately sad life amid the drugs and eventual indiscriminate sex that preceded her inevitable suicide. Hers was an empty life.

I have no idea how profitable and loving her relationship once was with her first husband, Alan Dobie. I knew him barely at all. He was a good actor who had a distinctive voice that worked for and against him. I can only say that he was one of only three or four actors who, in no way fawningly, sent me a letter saying he approved of one particular notice of mine, in which I had been less than overflowing in referring to his performance. In other words he accepted and even acted upon my constructive criticism. That was as welcome and appreciated as it was rare.

Peter O'Toole might allow me to claim an erstwhile friendship with him. We had both been newspaper copy-boys, him in Leeds and me at Yeovil. We shared a similar sense of fun, although I used to tell him he was better company, just the two of us together with a glass of Guinness, than when he felt he needed to camp things up a bit in a crowd of sycophantic followers from the Bristol Old Vic school.

His father was a footballer as well as a bookie. I heard from several that Peter wept openly in a Bristol side-street on the day of the Manchester United crash. But cricket was his sport and he eagerly went on taking tuition in the nets in later years. At his request, after he'd been playing Chekhov on a return to Bristol and had gone to watch some county cricket in Bath, I introduced him to Brian Close. His face was wonderfully expressive, that of a schoolboy.

I saw him when arguably he did some of his best work; that was in his Bristol Old Vic days as he worked hard on his discipline, attempted to cut back on his ale consumption, and tried to smash fewer cars. He never seemed to sleep. Theatregoers travelled miles to see him, not always in lead parts. He came round for supper, at times with pretty girls from the company. With my wife I drove him and Isobel, then a journalist girl friend, to Stratford in the newspaper's ropey Ford Pop, to see one of the tragedies.

Peter O'Toole
in his Bristol days

He played Hamlet at the age of 24 at the Theatre Royal. He lost even more weight as he rehearsed and seemed to be heading for a nervous breakdown. The company were so concerned about him that they cancelled a crucial late rehearsal. "Go off and forget all about the Prince. See how you feel tomorrow." I was much flattered when he turned up in my office (it was also where Isobel worked) and asked me to go off and have a few pints with him after work. It did him no harm. He may not have yet been fully ready to take on Hamlet but the applause was rightly warm and lasting. They liked him in King Street. The more conventional old fogeys just conveniently shut their ears to reports of the hairier stories.

The last time I saw him was at the funeral in Wales of Nat Brenner, such a key figure in the undulating and often stirring history of the Bristol Old Vic. The two of them had invariably discovered a potent creative brew. Their work in tandem was always a joy. Aspiring young actresses strolled the graveside for Nat's farewell, hoping to snatch a few treasured words with the actor. It was an occasion when he didn't want to be recognised. I experienced one slightly embarrassing moment, however. He saw me, the first time for a number of years, picked his way over the flowers and hugged me as the tears streamed down his face. And one young mourner, in a voice too loud and insensitive for immediate post-funeral sadness, turned to his friend and said: "Who the bloody hell is that? Looks like an out-of-work pro. May have appeared in something with Peter." Nat would have liked the irony of that.

My memories of O'Toole are many, like those of others who drank and laughed with him. I was really an occasional mate rather than a close friend and I certainly have no intention of including more than one personal story in these pages. He had gone up to the Garrick Theatre with the company to appear in the musical *Oh, My Papa!* which had a fetching score by Paul Burkhard. Peter's part, full of comedy, was that of a henpecked Uncle Gustave.

I had seen the show in Bristol and was sure it was going to run in London. It is possible I was influenced then by the sight of impresario Jack Hylton, sitting in the same row and making notes with the air of a man who sensed he spied a hit. Predictably, after some wise surgery in the script and minor changes to the cast, it opened in the West End. Here was a temporary change of direction and newly found commercial status for the Bristol Old Vic. Back in King Street, the accountants were prematurely totting up the anticipated revenue which should be coming west. The excitement was tangible.

But petty gallery politics were simmering away. The pre-show rumours suggested that an organised clique would be noisily antagonistic to the musical and those involved in its presentation. And the coachloads of loyal Bristolians in the audience sat in stunned horror and disbelief as the booing and hissing started in the gallery the moment the show ended. It was brutal, full of contempt for *Oh, My Papa!* The unequivocal demonstration took many of us completely by surprise. There were sexual as well as merely theatrical politics at work.

The curtain was rapidly brought down and some in the confused audience walked out, mystified by the outrageous behaviour from that vocal faction up in the gallery. Others reacted with a regional fervour that some aged pundits felt was as rare as it was gratifying. They started applauding composer Burkhard, director Warren Jenkins and the cast. It lasted for seven minutes, causing a dramatic rethink backstage. Up went the curtains again; Laurie Payne, Rachel Roberts, Sonia Rees and Peter O'Toole among others sang their hit numbers again. The gallery rebels, so well organised, now succumbed. I realised this was a news story, in addition to a first-night show, so went in search of the cast. "I so nearly burst into tears, fearing that the show was a flop," Rachel Roberts told me. Then her Celtic fire emerged. "I just wanted to shout back at the demonstrators." Jenkins and Burkhard just couldn't understand what had happened. O'Toole was typically succinct. "I'll catch up with those bastards."

He proposed that I should trail along with him, presumably for the rest of the night. I explained that I was duty-bound to catch the last train back to Bristol. After all, I had an eight-month pregnant wife with me. We'd already had enough unexpected drama for herself and our new baby for one day.

O'Toole's last words to me were: "You'll regret it." As a one-time aspiring newspaper reporter he possessed a sharp journalistic instinct. And there was Irish fire in his nostrils.

Bleary-eyed, I was in the office by 8 a.m. I'd written on the train my glowing review of the show and my account of the inflamed shenanigans which emanated from the gallery at the Garrick. A colleague greeted me: "Done well to get in so early after all that rumpus."

"How did you know about it?"

"Got it on the PA (Press Association) half an hour ago. Here, have a look at this."

It told me that Peter O'Toole was due in court at Clerkenwell later that morning, charged with being drunk and disorderly in Holborn at 2.10 a.m. He'd been with his sister who with domestic affection had refused to let go of him when he was forcibly put into a police van.

The court case which followed later in the morning claimed he had been shouting in a very loud voice. "Yes I was tight but not disorderly," he argued, adding descriptively that he had gone through several stoneware beakers of home-made mead. He was fined a nominal ten shillings and I was sorry that I had to leave him so that I could catch the last train home. But as he said in those parting words to me: "You'll regret it."

There was, too, I must admit, rather a lot to regret when it came to visiting the Bristol Hippodrome to see *Meet Mr Tombs*, a new farce by a Welshman called Richard Lawrence Griffith. It was a dreadful play, and the various local critics said so with considerable vitriol. I could find precious little to praise apart from the bountiful cleavage of ash-blonde actress Vera Day, whose flighty role at least allowed for a generous geographical tour of her bodily contours, if not exactly providing a test of her farcical range on stage. Within hours of our paper appearing, the author was writing to the editor. "The general opinion in this city is that your theatre critics are a lot of silly, stupid, petty frustrated writers. The people who have seen my play laugh their heads off." That was how he started his letter of wrath and he didn't subside. It caused me recently to exhume my yellow, festering review. I described the play as 'bitty, unfunny, cliché-ridden' – and that was only in the first paragraph. I have always considered myself a gentle, sensitive, probably gutless critic, pussyfooting with benign care over my choice of phrase. Mr Griffith, whose first play this was, showed no willingness to forgive us what he saw as the banal excesses of our trade.

My news editor pondered the author's letter which had been passed to him. "This is one for Mr Stoppard. I think we'll let him loose on this Mr Griffith fellow. There's mileage in the brimstone."

Tom had recently joined us from the *Western Daily Press*. Reg engaged him over lunch at Marco's Italian restaurant – where prices were kept reassuringly low for actors and journalists – and said he wanted him to write features and to turn out a weekly motoring column. The fact that young Stoppard couldn't drive a car was a minor consideration. "I'll concentrate on the upholstery," he's said to have told Reg with endearing spontaneity.

During my news days with the *World* I would on Friday mornings see and sit next to Stoppard in Flax Bourton Court, not far from his home in Long Ashton on the outskirts of Bristol. He was apt to read a Penguin paperback during the succession of trifling motoring offences and then pick up a summary of the better cases and the verdicts from the other reporters as we shared a half or two at the nearby Jubilee Inn during the lunch break. It was a dangerous practice, not so far from litigation if Tom's relayed evidence got mangled in transfer. But, as I remember, he had a decent shorthand and kept his reports short to avoid too many crucial facts becoming distorted and inaccurate.

He moved on a different cerebral level and would wander off in the middle of a conversation as a philosophical aside took his fancy. His hair was thick and unruly, his voice touched by an intriguing sibilance. Above all, he loved the theatre. The Theatre Royal was his spiritual home. His backstage friends allowed him to station himself in the wings. By acute observation, he learned the technical glossary of the stage. He knew and worshipped actors like O'Toole. They in turn liked him; they also sensed an exceptional, original talent impatient to burst free, as he juggled with words and dramatic situations. We at times played cricket together, he a gangling wicket-keeper with a dry glove-man's humour and notable intuition in quickly picking up the varying flights of the ball.

The unconventional interview with the writer of *Meet Mr Tombs* was absolutely right for him. He began by telling the readers that Mr Griffith was hopping mad. "Well, you can see his point of view. He has backed, written, produced, directed, cast, acted in and composed the music for a play which has been roundly summed up by the Bristol critics as a flop, embarrassing, tedious, witless, artless, vulgar, depressing, unfunny, cliché-ridden, plodding, lecherous and laboured …"

Tom must have been in danger of running out of adjectives – and he'd only just started. I don't know if he still remembers his collision course with Mr Griffith. He has written or watched hundreds of plays since his date with Mr Tombs. He may even have worked that Hippodrome-based episode into one or two of them.

I have a cowardly bent and don't like being confrontational with actors and directors, however fragile their egos. They do complain and we used to take it in turn to field their complaints when they stormed to the nearest phone. I remember having to persuade Frankie Vaughan to calm down when he took exception to something slipped into our diary. Dickie Dawson, a Canadian comic who for a time looked after Diana Dors' personal needs, was even more outraged about something we'd written about her stage persona. "What are you all – a load of puffs?" he thundered during a long-lasting tirade which clearly cast unreasonable doubts over our private practices.

The theatre has been an eventful, rewarding, at times exasperating, part of my professional life. For 22 years I was a regional critic for the *Guardian*.

That included dutiful visits to isolated village halls to see and squirm at self-indulgent plays by fringe companies, as well as the hundreds of plays I saw and enjoyed at Bath, Cheltenham, Swindon and, of course, Bristol. I never lost my sense of excitement as I drove to these performances. I make no claims about any singular academic zeal or profundity I brought to them. Yet seldom did I lose my village-boy enthusiasm. The *Guardian* subs changed little. Some of them were marvellously jolly and civilised, finding time to discuss the quality of the local real ales, even when edition time was approaching. My opinions were for the most part trusted. Very briefly I felt I was a victim of a feminist cell on the *Guardian's* arts-page desk and they made it obvious that they preferred a member of their own uncompromising gender to look after an idea I had put up as a potential feature. But that was infrequent and it could be, I partly imagined, the combined strident voice. As a freelance, as I was by that time, I did win a couple of moral battles. Well, struggling freelances needed to.

My taste in matters theatrical freely ranged across the intellectual, liberal and down-market scale. I was probably not an average critic. My stage scholarship was inclined to be scratchy. I disliked the profession's double standards – the way that the directors got away with all those libidinous and physical liberties as well as robust asides in some Shakespeare and the Restoration plays. Not that I was remotely a prude. What irritated me was the manner some audiences, staid and proper by nature, relished dubious lines and actions if they were discreetly wrapped up in the 'respectable' aura of classical drama.

I have had the privilege of seeing so much, instinctively reacting to so much, chuckling at so much. What has entertained me most of all? My answer may come as a considerable surprise. How I would have regretted missing the final years of music-hall. It was stiflingly tatty. By then its performers had become weary-eyed and cynical. The seats were threadbare; you could smell the dust and listen to the tin of the depleted pit orchestra. Torn sheet music had never been completely swept up from the crevices in the dank corners of the stalls. The dressing rooms retained the stench of redundancy. The saucy pencilled messages of forced bonhomie from generations of one-time top-of-the-bill comics had survived as metaphors of defiance and goodwill, still scratched in the plaster next to the discoloured wash basins, into which the occupants had once urinated in seedy ritual after the last house on Saturday nights.

And yet I treasured it with deep affection. In former years I had sat in mesmeric awe as the best of the comedians could, without prop or partner, hold an audience with all the compelling presence of one of those celebrated

Shakespearean actors from down the road in King Street measuring the consonants and cornucopia of emotions in sumptuous soliloquy.

On many Monday nights, clutching my press ticket, I had seen, admired and eavesdropped on so many of the finest that Variety had to offer. Backstage, we were expected to augment our review with a few appropriate quotes from the star. This was where I listened to the earthy, non-stop wisdom of Max Miller, the generosity of my favourite, Jimmy James ("Don't bother about me – give this young lad a lift instead. His first week, you know. Name of Roy Castle. You'll be hearing more about him.") There, on those Monday nights, first house, I found Vic Oliver grumpy, George Formby desperately tired – it was to be his final engagement – Old Mother Riley and her daughter Kitty arguing violently (that happened all the time, I was told), Terry Thomas being needlessly punctilious and making a fuss about the hyphen left off his name in the big posters. And toothy Tommy Steele, chirpy and unsophisticated, telling me: "You want a word with the feller who writes all my songs. Come across to the Royal Hotel in the morning, 11 o'clock. Ask for me." And so I did. His song writer was Lionel Bart, still in bed when I called. He too often seemed a wasted and unfulfilled talent to me, hardly helped by self-destructive tendencies. But I got a reasonable interview as his tormented head poked out from the sheets.

Such experiences were for me rich and instructive. Just like my consciously determined effort to learn more about, even write for, television. At TWW, forerunner of HTV, I shared an office with Guy Thomas, principal interviewer, personality and news reader every tea time. He was an urbane figure who later earned a reputation as a theatrical historian. A group of us went out most days for a pub lunch in his car. Gossip was confidentially imparted. The structural arrangement of the company, with most of its business being conducted impersonally in London, was far from satisfactory. Indeed, TWW was the first victim of a deliberate shake-up.

But I learned the language and technical ritual of television. Simultaneously I derived some modest encouragement. I wrote half-hour scripts for a Vivian Ellis profile and did another half-hour on *Salad Days*. In the process I had a lengthy radio interview with Julian Slade, a helpful, diffident music-maker whose notes were always going to be too "tinkly" for any real commercial success. The interview was for BBC Radio Bristol, another source of necessary freelance labours in those impoverished months. Local radio was a notoriously frugal employer. My interview, for all of 20 minutes of air-time, brought me a cheque for £10.

The following week I happened to see Julian Slade again and said how well he had done in the interview. Apart from his intermittent royalties I don't suppose he was earning much then. Almost jokingly I said: "They only paid me £10, you know. How about us sharing?" I pulled a crumpled note from my pocket and handed him £5. Without too much reluctance he accepted. It must have been the poorest return he ever received and it was just as well his agent was never told.

Perhaps I was affected in my act of generosity by a gesture of rare and kindly showbiz good-heartedness that came back to me from my Monday nights in the seductive tattiness at the Hippodrome, when the whiff of rancid fried onions reached up from Denmark Street and part-time musicians struggled to hit the right note.

We were coming to the end of the week and for comic Freddie Bamburger the end of a decidedly sluggish box-office. His unpretentious bit of sparingly rehearsed showtime was also coming to the end of its short run. No-one in the company, I suspect, was too sorry. But I felt genuinely sorry for Bamburger, a decent singer and old-style patter funny man with a contrived awfulness at the piano. It was all too smutty, however, even for the spattering of half-slumbering, beery members of the audience. Just as well the stage was crowded with semi-nudes, few of them appearing to know what they were supposed to be doing, except pout and expose superfluous flesh.

My review must have been relatively charitable. Soon I had Bamburger on the phone to my newspaper office. He asked to speak to me. He called me David and there were no introductory flourishes of affected affability. "Great, David, great! The best notice we've had on our run. I'm only sorry you didn't come on one of the earlier weeks – I'd have used your words in our publicity."

What was coming next? "Can't let it pass, David, without a bloody thank-you." (Oh dear, was this corruption coming up?) "We're going to have an end-of-tour party at the café next door after the final show. And I'd like you to come as my guest." There was perhaps a sly music-hall coding in his husky tones, but it was too subtle for me.

I turned up at the caff on the Saturday night, after covering Bristol Rovers. It would have seemed rude and ungrateful to ignore Freddie's unexpected invitation. Looking round the cramped restaurant, with the HP sauce bottles still on the tables, I spied the six nudes from the show. They had scraped off their make-up and suddenly looked very ordinary and unglamorous. They also looked bored as if they needed an early night. Freddie's party lacked much spark. Conversation was non-existent. Then he arrived and the girls went quiet and as obedient as a classroom of 12-year-olds. He came straight over to me. "Ah, David, nice of you to turn up. But my plans for you haven't materialised. I've had a word with Pam (his partner on stage) and she assures me all those lovely birds of mine are lesbians. I just didn't know it. My agent found them for me. All bloody lesbians, I ask you. And I was hoping to give you a free choice of my lovely chorus girls for the rest of the evening, to thank you again for that smashing notice."

I thought again of Freddie's earlier words, not quite as perfunctory as I'd taken them to be, and what he apparently had been promising. In truth I had assumed it was to be a jolly showbizzy party with a few spontaneous acts and mutual handshakes. Outside the caff, after leaving early, I caught a taxi home to my wife. I just didn't need anyone, however well intentioned, feeling that a bit of pimping was a fair exchange for a felicitous review.

But what in honesty has been my theatrical highlight over a lengthy, variegated career? Dodging the understandable taunts of name-dropping, I must nominate my lucky interview with Noel Coward.

He had come to Bristol to supervise the rehearsals for his last musical, *Sail Away*, and I had gone, at my news editor's behest, in search of a word with The Master. One of the Coward aides had seen me lurking. "He's not talking to anyone today. Far too busy. Not a chance. You're wasting your time. Maybe we shall arrange a Press Day just before the opening." There was unbending authority in what he was saying. What he was implying, in less tactful fashion, was: "Clear off. You've got no right to be here in the Hippodrome stalls."

Over the years I had learned how to be resourceful. I hung around in the shadows of the auditorium. And suddenly, after a quarter of an hour, I saw a solitary figure seated in Row K (funny how you remember some things). From the cigarette holder, I knew who it was. But how did one approach him?

"Yes?" He had spoken first.

"I'm from the local evening paper. Will there be any chance of a short chat later on?"

He sized me up as he paused. "Why not now? The rehearsal seems to be going well enough without me. Come and sit down."

I had read of a long history of general rehearsal rows. If such an eminent and revered figure as Coward was specifically involved in any of those excesses of temperamental licence, I was no more than vaguely aware of them. He was full of charm. The consonants were clipped and deliberately fashioned, just as the impressionists of the day copied. It was all straight from one of those patriotic films of his, or the style he preened in front of the French windows in a West End drawing room set.

We chatted for 30 minutes. He put his hand on my knee. "Good to meet you, dear boy." Yes, even 'dear boy' in the style we only pretended he talked. Well, he did. I offered him good luck with the new show and slipped away. My notebook was suitably full as I slipped past his glaring aide who had worked so hard to steer me away.

It was, my friends assured me, an accolade to be treasured, for The Master to place and rest a hand on a stranger's knee like that. In fact, Coward was not half as camp as many who come with their mincing walks as part of the oppressive effeminate territory. Frankie Howerd once gave me a similar hand-on-knee treatment after bustling me into a taxi and sitting rather too close to me. I had seen him first in his dressing room to discuss his appearance in *Hotel Paradiso* and his future plans for Shakespeare's Bottom the Weaver in a season with the London Old Vic. On that brief taxi ride, I had been requested to take him to the pub where a few of the young male actors from the BOV School went, possibly to be picked up. Frankie Howerd, a lonely, talented, promiscuous man, was companionable enough. But I was glad when my mission as cruising advisor was completed and we got to the back-street boozer. I left him, strangely enlightened, in a small group of fawning young men.

An interview with Michael Miles
Not as bad as it looks. But it does suggest the late quizmaster was saying:
"Another impertinent question like that, Foot, and I'll black the other eye!"

I used to take part from time to time in an HTV arts programme.
This one was about Chester Himes, a brilliant writer (and ex-con)
who specialised in detective fiction and bold racial themes. The producer
decided to put me into character for a modest role in the profile.

10

THIS SPORTING LIFE

Which role from my potpourri of professional duties has brought me the most private pride? All have been inextricably linked to the business, simple and exciting, of putting words on paper – whether I have been seduced by the joyous, nostalgic rattle of compositors' hot metal or the intimacy of speaking into a microphone.

For years, the unadorned title of 'reporter' was the best beyond challenge. It carried its own ring of dramatic authority. "I'm a reporter now," I used to whisper to my mother. Job description was far more important to my delicate ego than the content of the grey, inanimate pieces that I then produced with formulaic efficiency for my weekly paper.

For a short time I was equally proud of my speed in snatching a pencil and fashioning the look of the *Pink Un*'s feature pages. Those were the days of blank page plans, transformed into esoteric designs that sometimes I thought wouldn't have shamed an architect in a hurry. So yes, I liked being seen as a sub-editor. And then came my thirty years as a drama critic – wow, that implied a sniff of real, slightly snobbish status.

I switched to sport, partly on a whim, while attracted by the idea that all those acres of objective prose might be coming to an end and that I would be allowed to express the occasional opinion of my own. The first times I saw my by-line, followed by 'Sports Writer' or even 'Cricket Correspondent', the sensation was verging on the orgasmic. As my opportunity to specialise in cricket – its county matches, wisdom of the old pros at whose feet I worshipped, the game's unrivalled subtleties – I realised that this was really all I wanted: just to be a cricket writer.

The first county match I saw, in the late 1930s, at my hometown ground of Yeovil, Robertson-Glasgow (or 'Crusoe') was in the press box, as I learned years later. I hadn't yet progressed to long trousers; only later would he become my literary idol. The second championship match, again at Yeovil though not at the same ground, was after the war. John Arlott was broadcasting from the comfort of a deckchair. He signed my scorecard and I contrived to sit a few yards from him, in front of the BBC's outside broadcast van.

By then I was an impecunious junior reporter, certainly not yet the paper's Cricket Writer. But as my scope for sporting journalism broadened, I revealed a masochistic streak by taking on too much unofficial freelance work on Saturdays. There was one idiotic exercise in journalistic greed (what, at 7s 6d from a sweatshop paper for a day's labours?) when I was experiencing a busy spell with local radio to supplement my normal weekend commitments. Radio Bristol enlisted me as a DJ for an hour before the kick-off at Ashton Gate. I stayed in their cubicle, blissfully ignorant of their transitory pop and studio-enhanced music, to provide half a dozen football flashes in each half, followed by a lengthy interview with the star man afterwards. That wasn't the half of it. I was covering the game for the *Sunday Express* and they needed the first of their two 450-word reports immediately on the final whistle. In addition, I had mindlessly taken on coverage for the northern evening paper whose interest was centred on the visiting team, of course. At the time, competition was intense among the freelances, not all of whom lived locally.

My friends in the press box were fully occupied. So when yet another order from a distant paper came in at the last minute, I knew I had to find an inspired solution. Mark, my son, whose career is in banking, volunteered to provide it. I squeezed him into the radio box alongside me. I had access to a phone and he was able to dictate half a dozen of my running reports to two papers, with maybe a few improvements to my frenetic syntax. The difficulty for him was reading my writing. Somehow we got through it. This was, in its modest way, a triumph of logistics and intermittent good fortune when at least half the incoming calls, all booked in advance, arrived approximately on time.

At the end of the match I snatched my interviews, satisfied the *Sunday Express*, placated the anxious sports editors in the north with copy which miraculously made their varying editions and … there was still one to go. I had been booked to cover the match for the BBC's *Sports Report* which went out at 5.30 p.m. The frantic, brilliantly compiled programme was introduced by Eamonn Andrews. I made it, arriving in the Bristol studio with a match report scribbled in the taxi. Just as well the public never know.

I can offer too many criticisms of my enforced working method, while at the same time taking secret pleasure at the surprising success rate. Much of a sports journalist's life is inevitably feverish and superficial. We don't have time to delve below that surface and verify who scored the muddled late goals, especially when the centre half is honestly insistent that it was really an own-goal. We need to cut corners.

That discursive, richly readable cricket writer Alan Gibson knew all about my faults. In a piece for *The Times*, based on the biography of the tragic Harold Gimblett, he wrote: "Foot has always been capable of high-class writing but, as an old friend, I have felt he left himself little time for it … In one respect he is rather like his hero. He has been reluctant to work seriously at his writing and I suspect would have been just as pleased knocking off his regular quota for the *East Coker Mercury & Advertiser* as he suspects Gimblett would have been just as pleased to hit his sixes for Watchet as England." He's probably right. I never rejected professional pride, however. The head-spinning bustle and constant need for flexibility were forever part of the physical and mental appeal and the fun.

My relationship with Gibson was warm and appreciative. He openly abused me in the press box and through the whisky fumes. He was an appalling cultural and intellectual snob, relishing the chance to take a public, pejorative swipe at me for any grammatical lapse or, worse, ignorance of Greek mythology, never taught at any of my schools. He could be a bad-tempered man and liked to pick a fight with gate-men and self-important club officials. But the climate improved, usually, as the whisky, often carried in a baby's bottle, softened his sinews and made him more amenable. He hobbled in plimsolls, still able to make a decent speed on his way to the bar. For my part I bundled him several times into my car as we attempted, with mixed success, to catch the train out of Weston-super-Mare for him after a fixture at Clarence Park.

I was intoxicated more by Alan Gibson's style than the content of his baby's bottle. He claimed he wasn't a journalist (something else that bothered me when newspapers and broadcasting were really his only source of employment). He wrote his reports in late afternoon, using a fountain pen which miraculously he never seemed to mislay. He would rely on a few equally boozy chums from the Stragglers Bar for an elusive fact on the day's play. The regular cross-reference to a match at The Parks in Oxford years before, when he was missing one of his many lectures, came straight from his infallible memory. As far as I recall, he never carried a reference book with him. But he didn't like to be distracted too much when it was time for him to start writing. "Bugger off – can't you see I'm busy?" he would say with irritated finality to an intruder. And then, as if consumed with guilt: "Oh, all right. If you want to do something useful, go and buy me a whisky."

Alan was a natural broadcaster, expressing his views with clarity as you'd expect from an ex-president of the Oxford Union. He was a member of the BBC's Test match commentary panel, some have said the finest, until a day of alcoholic excess led to his dismissal in 1975. It was a fearful psychological blow to him.

He could be extraordinarily kind and encouraging. When his BBC work had substantially dried up, he was asked by HTV to commentate on a match at the County Ground in Bristol. It was televised and he suggested to them that I should be his co-commentator, a completely new experience for me. I was flattered and was nervous as the first over approached. "Come on, David. Let's make it a nice civilised conversation, just as if we're having a chat over a drink in the BBC Club." Cheered by his words, I much enjoyed the half a dozen inserts that followed during the day. "Not so bad, was it? Let's hope we're asked again," said a delightfully relaxed Gibson. We weren't. HTV had no real budget for cricket, despite the enthusiasm of director Derek Clark who went on to produce an excellent documentary on Wally Hammond, disgracefully rejected by the network.

My virginal broadcast with the vastly more experienced Gibson reminded me of a previous, less successful broadcast involving both of us. Alan was due to cover for BBC regional radio a county game at Glastonbury. I was there to look after the match for my evening paper.

Suddenly in mid-morning a BBC engineer, in a much flustered state, came rushing out of the OB van. "God, we're on in two minutes and Alan hasn't even arrived yet. Can you stand in for him?"

I had never done a live commentary before, certainly not one without direction or basic notes. Half pushed, I was lowered into the only chair and cans were impressively positioned over my ears. "They'll talk to you back in the studio."

And they did. "Are you getting programme? Oh yes, should have asked – what's your name?"

Within 30 seconds, I heard myself being introduced on air. "And now to see how the opening overs are going, over to … David Frost."

Well, it didn't bother me at all that they got the name wrong. More important to me was that I could see the scoreboard though the steamy window – and that my team, Somerset, were batting. I could recognise Merv Kitchen and Roy Virgin. Tensely, I kept it going for a quarter of an hour.

I never quite found out what happened to Alan Gibson that Saturday morning. But it led to other regular sports broadcasts, in cricket and football, for me.

No other sport carries so rich and luxuriant a tapestry as cricket. It isn't simply the intricacies of the game itself, its ritual and its drollery. It's the people who have always played it – with their freshly creased flannels and funny hats of iridescent shades, their singular ability to convey a pastoral afternoon in a village of sunshine. It remains nowadays, however, a defiant act of preservation as it faces up to the apparent horrors of cricket's evolving structure which now encompasses such a confusing array of competitions, countries and fluctuations, making most of us wonder which day the game is starting – and how many days it is being played.

Cricket at its loftier and haughtier level is now about administrators in smart suits, mushrooming buildings, Asian bookmakers, PR consultants and some county clubs with more staff advisors and fitness specialists than there are overs in a day. Everyone tells us the changes are necessary and life-saving as football increasingly takes over in plutocratic greed. We witness helplessly but with some sympathy as our traditional cricket gets sucked into the global oscillations. But is it more than merely pointless and romantic on my part that I still eagerly pull in the car and find myself watching a village match on its carpet of buttercups and fading dreams?

The game of cricket will never cease to be my favourite, whatever the now unceasing radical experiments and bureaucratic confusions. Nor will village cricket ever fail to be for me the most pleasurable of all. Helmets have turned up intrusively under the sycamores and the glib jargon of the changing first-class scene has dared to reach our sporting meadowlands. Yet the gentle memories and timeless tableaux remain, too endearing to be forgotten.

As devotees we used to travel, no doubt illegally, to away matches in a sawmills lorry. There were no sides and the layers of sawdust blew furiously into our eyes. We would habitually arrive like cricketers from a blind school. Our enthusiasm would be quickly restored, just like our eyesight. In the outfield, we slithered in the cow pats, unable to save ourselves from such indignity. Fat, jolly farmers did the umpiring, with minimal qualification, until milking-time.

For one visit to Evershot – I'd been recently promoted from our 2nd XI ("You'm only picked because thee's can bowl straight") – I took 7-6. The skipper's pre-match words had not been the most morale-elevating ones to say to someone who pretended he was an off-spinner. Bowling at times seemed to go round in rotation. My supposed ability to aim frugally for the stumps found me opening the attack. They were the best figures of my undulating career, not achieved, it must be said, without incident. Our umpire, normally the wicket keeper, was Bill Stroud, a good friend of mine. He turned down only one of my lbw appeals. The reaction of the Evershot batsman to another assured shout of expectation from me led to a lengthy confrontation with Bill who, when the home player refused to leave, simply lay on the ground and lit a Woodbine. The delay of nearly ten minutes, after insults and threatening oaths had been expended, merged eventually to comic, silent surrealism more suited to Beckett's *Waiting for*

Godot. When the match re-started, I completed my over. I didn't appeal again – and nor did I take another wicket. My bowling feat was rightly not expunged from the scorebook. As far as I know, it still stands as one of East Coker CC's more modest post-war records.

After the match, the antagonism evaporated as we shared a Dorset ale with the Evershot team at the Rest and Welcome. Grievances were very rarely harboured in village cricket, not in the years that I played, anyway. My more immediate concern now was to work out how I might pick up the interminable list of prize-winners and stall-holders – names were the omni-present lifeblood of my weekly – from the Women's Institute secretary, Winnie, next morning. The new fixture with Evershot had awkwardly clashed with East Coker's annual flower show. Not an easy choice in the moral or practical sense for me. But I was soon well aware I'd tackled the dilemma as any bright-eyed teenager with a spinner's loop should have. Flower show results were all very well in the context of good-natured parochial competition. I had, though, made the right decision, I felt certain, in plumping for an afternoon busily, if controversially, employed taking all those unlikely wickets in tandem with my mate, Bill.

It was still a complicated operation. I had already added an element of justifiable fiction in my earlier approach to Winnie. "Can I rely on you? There are so many fetes and flower shows on Saturday. If your husband, Arthur, wins the cup for the most successes, I'll make sure he's mentioned at the top of the column." That bit of family flattery was a sure bet – Arthur always won the cup.

I cycled to her home on the Sunday morning, stepping over the prize marrows and huge onions at the back door. Dutifully I took down all those names. And it seemed as if I was filling half a dozen reporters' notebooks. It was a wearisome, mechanical process, not remotely creative or taxing. Fibbing wildly, I said how much I regretted not being able to attend.

On the Tuesday morning it was my turn in the office to open the editorial mail. One, addressed to the sports editor, was a village correspondent's short account of the match between Evershot and East Coker. It stated that a young journalist had been the star, taking seven cheap wickets and being twice on a hat-trick. No mention of the batsman who wouldn't walk. But my vanity was touched. Well yes, 7-6 wasn't bad. I instantly wondered whether Wally, the sports editor, would want to give the match a special cross-head. In the next breath, I feared the consequences if my surreptitious cricket appearance was exposed. Vanity would have to be sacrificed.

I pulled out my fountain pen and reluctantly blotted out any reference to this young journalist who fancied himself a bit with his off-breaks.

My cricket was still restricted because of my work. In truth I wasn't much of a player. I possessed a good-looking cover drive, which had ensured me a place in my school's first eleven for two years. I was of a nervous disposition, fearful of being faced by an exquisite yorker first ball. From school days I was discouraged from making strokes to leg. I could bat instinctively, more often out to catches than bowled. My late cut was a privilege I occasionally allowed myself. I was more enamoured by my modest bowling (an older man's Vic Marks, my pals used to joke). I could keep a length and essay variety. But as a genuine spinner – despite the persevering advice given me by that lovely Somerset rascal Bill Andrews – I produced little real turn and was not risked when sloggers with expansive reaches were on top.

I liked captaining my side. For several years I ran a Sunday team, the Bristol Badgers. We had no ground and no kit. But we compiled a rather impressive fixture list and, in my case, a valuable facility to recruit players on the previous night. Many of the Bristol City and Bristol Rovers players willingly turned up. Some of them were on the county groundstaff; they all loved their cricket, free of football's rigid disciplines. On occasions I also slipped in good cricketers from the local counties' 2nd XIs. Oppositions rather disapproved of my flexible team selection methods so in some cases I would consciously avoid names from the county staff being mentioned too often.

An assortment of cricketers, footballers, actors and journalists, even a policeman, taking the field at Weston-super-Mare, 1975

At least once a summer, I would captain a journalists' team against the Bristol Old Vic. Peter O'Toole led the thespian contingent, well watered and full of Shakespearean flourishes, in one much-quoted encounter. He really did come in from third man to bowl critic John Coe with his first ball. It was a pre-destined gesture, as if the gangly, loose-limbed actor of such talent and extrovert traits was paying back John for what were perceived as too many tepid notices.

In a later fixture Leonard Rossiter was the actors' skipper. His personality was diametrically opposed to that of O'Toole. Rossiter was a natural sportsman, once a decent footballer and now seen as a dour slow left-arm bowler. Unlike O'Toole, he had little to say. He took the game seriously and there were few outward signs of his considerable skills as a comic actor. As opposing captains we shared drinks afterwards but conversation was not easy. In that similar role O'Toole had transformed the match into the kind of dominant, ever-funny performance that wicket-keeper Stoppard later wrote and talked endlessly about.

Very soon after this, my beloved evening paper had folded. Nothing could have been more predictable. Circulation had nose-dived and the *Evening Post*, which by now pulled all the boardroom strings, was ready to get shot of it. At Colston Avenue, Northcliffe House was, of brutal necessity, chronically short of staff and space, and it waited helplessly to discover when the *World* would cease to print. The news came on a late Saturday afternoon in 1962. The staff were asked to gather in the canteen and the bland statement was soullessly read to them. "It was the most dreadful experience of my life," said Barbara Buchanan, one of the *World*'s exceptionally talented writers and award-winners.

I was grateful to miss that melancholy meeting. Instead, I was covering City's game at Halifax. The Shay, where several years before I'd seen pram wheels protruding through the terracing and had fallen in love with all the signs of such crumbling dignity, wasn't for me a bad place to say my goodbye. For convenience I hitched a lift back on the team coach to Bristol.

Invited to join the club and the players for an evening meal at a hotel in Buxton, it turned into something of a wake. Fred Ford, the City manager, the warmest-hearted of old-style football bosses, suddenly got up as we all finished our apple tart. "Right, then. Quiet for a moment. Now some of you may have heard that the *Evening World* has closed. So no more David Foot with his fair reports, kidding us he's seen the same game as us. But we'll miss him. Now I want you buggers to get on your feet and drink a toast to him and his paper."

It could have been slightly mawkish. I was sitting next to my mate and rival Peter Godsiff. Out of habit, I'd just checked on the goal-scorers, even if I didn't need that functional information for any more Monday follow-up reports. The players were all standing, offering their obligatory digs and personal jokes which they liked to trade. Pro footballers could be exuberant in insult but the reporters liked to think it was offered in affection. After that we had a brief spontaneous song or two, with Alex Tait, schoolteacher-turned-centre forward, and myself taking it in turn in discordant jollity at the hotel's off-key piano. I thanked dear old Fred – and then it was back to Ashton Gate in time for David Coleman.

I chose to freelance, though for some time precariously. A hint or two of risk always appealed to me. There was, encouragingly, scope for more writing about cricket. I got on well with the players; we were roughly the same age and confidential chats were easier because of it.

In later years, as an older figure, that kind of rapport was much more elusive. Andy Caddick appeared quite defensive when I tried once for an easy-going interview. So was Courtney Walsh. I was a great admirer of Mark Lathwell and thought he and Marcus Trescothick would be opening together for Somerset for years. Mark withdrew whenever there was a camera in sight and hated the public commitments of communication in being a county cricketer.

The first time I went to see Marcus at his home, this chubby, uncomplicated lad of sixteen or so called to his mother: "Put the kettle on, Mum, and make our visitor a cup of tea." He was full of courtesy and youthful helpfulness. Then he, too, for every understandable reason, seemed to go into a shell. The barrier was too readily put up whenever a reporter, often with no intent to write about him, hovered in innocence. That wasn't merely an off-shoot of his mental stresses. The bad old days, when the tabloids bared their teeth as they looked for and at times created sensationalism, have gone. It is time for the county clubs, especially those with a persistently wary record, to take a warmer and more trusting attitude. The county scene is full of new faces, or dare I say strangers? And the press boxes are sadly just as unfamiliar to me. Too often we sense a barrier between the players and those who write about them. How often do we see players and press having a drink together, as once they did? Come to that, how often do the players sit and chat over a pint with the public? County cricket is in danger, perhaps irretrievably, of losing for ever that cosy erstwhile affinity.

My interest in first-class cricket has invariably centred on the person rather than the player. I have tended to write about Gimblett and Wally Hammond because both were complex sportsmen. Books gave me the chance and the space to explore their tormented psyches. As I have frequently written, cricket attracts the morose and the introspective like no other sport. We need only to ponder the long list of suicidal players that writer David Frith has so painfully compiled.

There have never been more gifted cricketers in our various county competitions, many of them seduced – as part of the new breed of mercenaries – by the relative pots of gold somehow conjured up by threadbare clubs. Nor have there been, just as significantly, so many grey, seemingly vacuous or defensive players. Some seem mentally imprisoned by the strictures and unrelenting disciplines of the modern game. Where is the personality spark to re-enlighten them?

In its headlong rush to keep up with cricket's changing attitudes, cricket has lost its zest and its soul.

I first met Viv Richards soon after he came to this country to quality for Somerset. Len Creed, a cheerful, bucolic bookmaker from Bath on his way to becoming the county chairman, had been to the Caribbean on holiday and returned with this unknown batsman from Antigua. His words to me tumbled out in uncontrolled enthusiasm.

"He's going to play for Lansdown while he qualifies. I'm telling you he's the best young batsman in the West Indies. And he wants to play for us. Come to Bath and I'll introduce him to you. At the moment I've got him rolling the square at the Lansdown ground – but I'm not sure he likes that too much. It's all a bit strange to him. Vivian is quite a shy lad, well brought up. Used to sing in the Cathedral choir, you know."

In fact, Len couldn't have been more solicitous to the newcomer. He told me, with one of his confidential asides, that he had even remembered Viv's fleshly needs and sorted out a girl friend for him. In a matter of weeks Richards was crashing the ball about in all directions for his new club, so much so that one or two oppositions were murmuring that he should be discreetly omitted from the team. In other less coded words, he was too good for the standard, not by any means a negligible one, that Lansdown were used to.

I went to meet IVA and found him then as quiet and restrained as Len had suggested. Over the years that followed we chatted on boundary benches or in secluded corners of the bar. Others said that he possessed a fiery temperament, particularly when roused by a racial slur. I'm sure that was true, although I saw little evidence of it in our relationship. Possibly I knew instinctively which subjects to avoid.

Quickly I marvelled – never in an obsequious way – at his exceptional prowess. I simply accepted that he would go on to play for the West Indies. This was well before his stormy departure from Somerset, along with that of Joel Garner and Ian Botham, of course. In the summers when first we chatted openly together, he was idolised in the dressing room. He was a match-winner. More than that, he was held in affection. Young pros would look at him with eyes of admiration and say to me, "Just look at him" as he snoozed against a coffin. "Probably out with 'Both' last night. But he'll wake up in a minute and score a hundred." And he did, as the weariness made way for the clips through mid-wicket. Some of those mischievous shots may have looked too recklessly irresponsible in less expert hands. He made those inclinations of unorthodoxy something to savour.

I used to write and broadcast a regular review about West Indian cricketers in this country for the BBC's Caribbean service. It often included a taped interview with one of the players. By now, Viv's feats and burgeoning progress were an animated talking point, not least back in St John's, Antigua. I had to work to persuade him to be interviewed. He was nervous and there was much editing, with tape and razor blades, before I sent that first piece featuring him 'up the line'. He rapidly improved and my improvised editing sessions were less necessary. I encouraged him to offer the occasional contentious viewpoint on an issue of the day – and to slip in quaint folksy sayings from his home parish.

The shy, taciturn Viv Richards gave way to an international cricketer of confidence and what some saw as the signs of arrogance in his slow, swaggering walk to and from the crease. He assured me it was a mistaken judgement.

My most intimate time with him was on the evening at Taunton after he'd scored 322 against Warwickshire in 1985. It was a wonderful innings with as much grace as muscle. He made the Warwickshire bowlers look risibly ordinary. There was a brutality about his batting, though he never demeaned it by any ugly liberties. It was one of the days that he arrived at the ground, visibly in need of the good night's sleep after, one imagines, too many distractions.

More than an hour after the end of the day's play, by which time most of his team-mates had showered and gone home, I tentatively went in search of him. He took so long over his toiletry and deodorising rituals that he was always the last player to leave the dressing room. There he was, still wrapped in his towel, sitting alone on the bench. No suggestion of celebration or self-acclaim. He had already acknowledged as he came off the field the cheers of the doting supporters, some of whom had come across from the cattle market and stayed to be enraptured, leaving the drovers to load the lorries.

He was tired and reflective. He beckoned me to join him and he found champagne which he poured into plastic mugs. In his own way he was now ready quietly to celebrate. The dressing room was deserted apart from us. And for nearly another hour we talked, our conversation deflecting across unscheduled territory. Viv would never have claimed, I suspect, that he rated notably high in intellectual matters; he was more inclined to leave those more profound affairs to the cerebral Peter Roebuck – in the days, that was, that they were still speaking to each other and in awe of their differing skills. Now, in a smelly dressing room strewn with discarded kit, he unwound. There was no prompting needed from me. I had never seen him so eager to talk and I'm not sure he ever was again in his bountiful life of sport.

A few hours earlier he had scored a triple hundred, so powerful and consummate that one experienced Warwickshire player, in my hearing, said he would give up the game for ever as he realised the enormity of the gulf between them. Now, in the stillness of a cricket ground after almost all the players had gone home, IVA was ready to evaluate what he had achieved. But it had nothing at all to do with cricket.

His innings, indeed, was barely mentioned. Nor was cricket in general. To my surprise he moved onto religion instead. He also talked of his school friends he continued to see whenever he returned to Antigua. He talked lovingly of his family and the influence they had on him. He chuckled as he recalled his days as a waiter, balancing the glasses with a slip fielder's dependable hands. It was a contemplative and spiritual journey that he chose spontaneously to make. It certainly wasn't remotely what I had expected.

In 1979 I had ghosted the first of his autobiographies. By then I was fully aware of his sublime gifts of batsmanship and suspected that before long some writer, here or abroad, would be wanting to write Viv's life story. It was not intended to be a pretentious tome of literature but I felt that his early impact, now as a memorable Test cricketer, was well worth putting permanently on paper. I found a publisher who agreed. The problem for me, by than a busy freelance, was the commitment. I was given three weeks to write the book.

Viv, although keen to be helpful, was not adept at anecdote or specific recall. So off I went to the Central Library in Bristol for a day. It would ensure, I argued, that at least I knew something about Antigua and its

365 beaches. I read what I could about Nelson's links with the island. I corresponded with wife-to-be Miriam. In my early research I snatched chats with my subject whenever I could. We sat on boundary seats, Viv padded-up and ready to go in next. We had our one tiff when he failed to turn up at my home for an arranged session on a day when Somerset weren't playing. I made contact late that day after many phone calls. Against my nature, I went for him. I knew he valued family life so hesitantly I played my sentimental card.

"Vivian, we may as well call the whole project off. You know how little time I have to spare and I desperately needed to see you today." Then, with some justification, I brought my family into the necessary rebuke. "My wife had prepared a special West Indian lunch for you (true) and my children, Mark and Julia, have been waiting all day with their autograph books (equally true). And you've let them down."

It worked – as it simply had to, with now just a fortnight left. There was one more day free from cricket. Viv motored to Bristol and spent the day running through the highlights of his career and detailing the incident, in the match between Antigua and St Kitt's, when he was banned for not walking. The raucous row, involving 6000 spectators and their ultimatum 'No Vivi, No Play' remains a much-quoted talking point. It should be added that my wife's cookery was enjoyed and our two children got their autographs. The book marginally met the deadline.

Richards was inevitably worked into many of my match reports; it would have been difficult to avoid the mentions. Some of his best innings were at Taunton where the boundaries are short, letting him multiply his sixes as if they were delicate golf chips. The cars in the adjacent park were never safe. Nor were groundsman Cec Buttle's runner beans or the tombstones, crouching in St James's churchyard like intrepid close fielders. The *Guardian* generously encouraged individuality when there was space to spare. I was still surprised when 'Crumpet and Cricket' topped one of my Somerset reports. The good-natured levity was justified by the mood of my copy although I can only assume the headline writer had been jocularly affected by a previous stint with the red-tops.

Taunton saw some mighty and explosive cricketers. I often watched fellow Yeovilian, Botham, excel and retain vividly the image of him pointedly changing direction after his dismissal, to confront a vociferous and boorish member. I saw Richards, eyes blazing, take on a Yorkshire bigot at Clarence Park. I wondered how close Roebuck, seen as a cold fish, actually got to the captaincy of his country. Once he gave me a highly readable interview saying that he was quitting cricket to become, he hoped, a politician. Next morning, just before I dictated the story to London, he phoned me to say he'd had second thoughts and pleaded with me not to use the piece I had just finished writing.

Cricket writing was always to me more about the man than his runs. I chased Tom Graveney across golf courses to try to discover the volume of his disaffection for Tom Pugh, the Old Etonian who was being brought in to lead Gloucestershire at Tom's expense. Stamina too often came into the job. I spent days chasing round the country trying to locate that lovely Pakistan batsman, Zaheer Abbas, the subject of another of my ghosting exercises. Apart from any other considerations, I had no journalistic regrets at being held along with my wife at gunpoint in Lahore. Who rightly says that the most enthralling sport is away from the ground?

Nor did I have any qualms about my professional switch from news to sport. Human quirkiness encompasses both. The West Country had very few more stylish batsmen than Jack MacBryan, whose father ran a mental asylum. Jack used to admit to me that he was "a bad-tempered sod". He had a sweeping contempt for most of his fellow Somerset amateurs: "None of them can play – the most glowing compliment ever paid to me was that I reminded them of a Yorkshire professional." He went into the record books for the fact that, in his only Test match, against South Africa at Old Trafford, play was so curtailed that he failed to bat, bowl or field. I should perhaps have brought a rare smile to his lips by telling him I, too, had a single Test match. Editor Stephen Fay showed sympathy and with much kindness gave me an international for *Wisden Cricket Monthly*.

MacBryan used to top the Somerset batting averages and was a great source of background nuance for me when I visited him at his Cambridge home. He represented the county at rugby, golf and hockey, too. Life was not always smooth or rewarding for him. He was taken prisoner in the 1914-18 war and he went on to lose most of his money on the Stock Exchange. Yet he had been married to a Gaiety Girl and liked the company of a pretty woman.

He may have been a bit of a snob but he was a journalist's dream for nostalgic gossip. He was probably absolutely right about the starchy amateurs' factions in the segregated era in which he played. A pity he couldn't find a good word to say about many of them.

So MacBryan was a curmudgeon, however companionable he could also be on a good day. Everyone in the West Country agreed that he was worthy of greater recognition. In the cricket press box of that era, on rainy days, he could be a guaranteed subject for discussion and sharply varying viewpoint.

The press boxes were where professionally I was happiest. I found myself surrounded by well-fleshed mates who valued fellowship as well as the cricket. Our kinship came naturally. The humour, never far away, could be earthy as well as subtle. There was a bond that allowed us to share jokes, often at each other's expense, and profounder points about the match we'd been sent to watch and comment on. That was in the days, of course, when sports editors believed in decent coverage for championship fixtures, and the writers felt the word allocation justified their presence and judgement.

Our faces would light up when, at five to eleven on the first day, we discovered who from other papers would be sharing the box with us. We may not often have seen Jim Swanton too far from Canterbury but we held him in some esteem for his civilised enterprise in ensuring that the St Lawrence ground offered us a mid-morning drink. At more remote out-grounds, John Woodcock, most estimable and unassuming of fellow scribes, would lead the way to the beer tent. He liked the ritual of a pint at noon.

The tabloid boys had to write for their specific market. But from my experience, their affection for first-class cricket was no less marked. They affected to squirm at a slightly pompous sentence being dictated from another corner of the box. "Nice one – only wish we could get away with that on the *Mirror* and the *Sun*." Sometimes they were more than half serious.

It's hard to imagine that once cricket's press boxes were occupied by solemn-faced men in winged collars. They all looked like ageing non-conformist priests. They exchanged few words, preoccupied as they were by the verbose job in hand: recording not just every wicket to fall but every four cut off. The only sound from these po-faced chroniclers was the remorseless scratch of their fountain pens.

I couldn't have tolerated that. In the so much more relaxed days, we relished the lovely human mix of David Green, wondrously erudite as he quoted Hardy or a snatch of modern poetry, with a succession of bawdy memories from his time on the playing circuit.

We got on so much better as writers in our relationship with the cricketers. The bar tables groaned with stories, more than half of them authentic. Bomber Wells, Gloucestershire's much loved off-spinner, had hundreds of stories, many involving his participation. All Bomber wanted in return, apart from the laughter, was an increase in the membership of the Gloucester Labour Party.

His ceaseless dispensing of timeless anecdotes was only matched by the Somerset pair, Peter Robinson and Bill Andrews. Like the portly Wells, it was claimed that they had a wonderful, elongated story about every one of their contemporaries. Not that life was a guaranteed bundle of mirth for Bill, someone who suffered from concealed depression. I helped him with his autobiography and our greatest achievement was to shorten the Andrews word-count from 160,000 to 60,000. The trouble was that initially he'd written pages in his neat handwriting on every one of those jokes, all recounted without malice. He was an enthralling story-teller and, if the grammar was apt to falter a little, who cared?

Bill Andrews

That editing duty of length wasn't our greatest crisis. On the day Bill's book, *The Hand That Bowled Bradman*, was due to be sent to the printers, I took a phone call at five o'clock in the morning. "Something terrible's happened. Haven't slept all night. I think I got a few facts and tales wrong. I can't let it go – so I've decided to scrap the bloody book altogether. Can I leave it to you, David, to tell the publishers and printers?" He was adamant. I was fully aware of his fragile mental state and feared he might do something drastic. For the life of me I couldn't think of any incident that was libellous enough to pull a book only hours before it went into print.

I needed time to ponder what to do. Bill, in an advanced nervous state, remained completely unyielding. "Stay in bed, Bill. I'll be with you in half an hour." I motored frantically to his home in Weston-super-Mare. And I talked to him in alien marathon style, ignoring his protests. At last I convinced him that no-one had been defamed and there was nothing actionable in his stories. The book came out and, as a simple account of what life was like for a professional cricketer, it was warmly acclaimed. No-one heard of that last-minute scare.

When I return to towns where I used to watch county matches, I remember the routes by what remains of playing surfaces and phone boxes where I ad-libbed my clichés. Cricket grounds, even those now overgrown, keep their appeal for me. Some have been safety hazards. At Bristol some years ago, while renovations were being carried out, we had to climb into the lofty improvised box by scaling some scaffolding. It's hard to appreciate how that *Times* veteran Dick Streeton made the ascent with all those reference books he so rarely failed to bring with him.

The Nevil Road ground at Bristol, modernised and brightened, still looks forbiddingly grey because of the Victorian orphanages that partly encircle the playing area. This was the socially deprived city of long ago when children crammed the window sills for a treasured and envied glimpse of Grace and Jessop. I saw neither play, of course, but pretend that I did. I did see Arthur Milton many times, latterly propping his cycle against my gate as he delivered in succession the mail and then the papers. If I was on occasions awake as early as Arthur, we'd stop for a dewy morning chat. It would range from Highbury and the recent vagaries of the track at the County Ground to, not so predictably, the university education that eluded him.

At times the generations got slightly blurred: as when I talked to Tony Brown and Chris Broad and realised I'd played carefree evening cricket with their fathers back in the fifties. The privilege for me, still essentially a village boy, was to find myself talking and drinking with my heroes. I know what it was like when Peter O'Toole met Brian Close for the first time.

And what was the true peak for me? Just standing, unobtrusively I hope, in the company of county players as they relived the frustrations of a day in the field, their spirits lifted by runs after tea. I got on well with Graham Burgess because of that contradictory 'courtly stroll in the outfield' … with another village lad, Mervyn Kitchen … with Harold Stephenson, with his wicket keeper's likeable cunning … with Jim Foat, the best fielder in the business … Ron Nicholls, the goalkeeper and opening bat with all the shots if only he'd used them more … Brian Langford, spinning away all day when you needed him to block one end … Tony Brown, blue eyes flashing when a boundary was carelessly sacrificed … David Allen, perhaps wondering why he was never captain. So many names. So much humanity to dwell on during bland winter evenings.

When I became one of the *Guardian*'s regular cricket writers, sent for the first time round the country, I realised I had no other ambitions left.

With my favourite wicketkeeper, Gloucestershire's Andy Wilson

*The launch of Ian Botham's benefit in Yeovil
(from left) Tony Brown, the author, David English, Ian Botham, Vic Marks*

11

WEAKNESS FOR SCANDAL

There is no reason why I should want to bask in the fact that I briefly met Neville George Clevely Heath, sadist and serial killer of attractive women. I was in my last year at grammar school and maybe a potential newspaper reporter's sense of unmitigated scandal was already lurking.

Leaning on my three-speed bike at the bottom of Hendford Hill, I was waiting for one of Yeovil's buses to come by. The hill was a long one and I had already perfected the technique, taught me by older schoolboy friends, of grabbing the luggage ladder as the unseeing driver slowed to change gear. It was a dangerous practice but we got away with it – and arrived home earlier for tea.

To my surprise, a man stopped to speak to me. It was an innocuous, commonplace conversation, cheerful and articulate. His appearance held my attention; he was wearing an expensive, well-cut suit and gave the impression of having an executive type of job. He was also strikingly good-looking with wavy fair hair and early hints, from what he said, that he was healthily heterosexual. I had been warned – and from cases I read about recently in the local paper – of single males who prowled in search of innocent prey.

This man, ten years or so older than me, had much charm. He said with a smile that he was lost and didn't know Yeovil at all well. And gradually his conversation changed in subject matter. What, he wanted to know, did this Somerset town have to offer? Where was there to go in the evening? A pretty young woman walked past, eyeing him up with admiration. "Well yes, I can also see that there are some decent lookers around. Not tarts, are they? That's what I like."

I wasn't quite sure what he meant. Tarts made me think of bramleys, not shorthand-typists with nice legs, on their way home from work. But he pursued his theme. It was drifting in a direction that made me feel uncomfortable. There was an assumption of sexual sophistication from him that only confused me. "I must be on my way," I stammered. At this distance I remember our Hendford Hill chat in graphic detail. As I moved off I looked back and saw him already talking to another girl he had stopped, I imagine, to ask for fictitious information. His face stayed vividly with me.

A few weeks later I saw it again – on the front page of the national papers as I perused them in the Reading Room as part of my daily ritual. I was transfixed. That was the handsome fellow who stopped to talk to me on my journey home from school, I told myself. I was in no doubt about it. And here he was, suspected of the murders of Margery Gardner and Doreen Marshall. A third murder, again horribly sadistic in the way it was committed, was soon being linked to Heath.

He was hanged by Albert Pierrepoint after an Old Bailey trial in 1946 laden with sensation and accounts of unutterable perversion. It emerged that much of his life had been clouded by skirmishes with the law, lies, borstal, courts martial and police convictions. He constantly used aliases including his make-believe title of Group Captain. It was revealed, too, that he was a fraudster who could charm with his glib composure. Some time later, in my early routine police station calls for the *Western Gazette*, I discussed my encounter with Inspector Gregory. "No-one, I'm sure, will believe me." The senior CID officer didn't laugh at me.

"I would," was his instant reply. "We had him on our files and he'd been knocking around the Yeovil and north Dorset area about the time you feel you saw him. Yes, I think it was Neville Heath."

The *Gazette* bristled at any murmur of sexual felony and its reporters were prudishly ordered to keep their notebooks deep in their pockets whenever there was a lurid story on the point of breaking. "Leave that to the *Mirror* and the *News of the World*. Not our line of country," the news editor would say in magisterial finality when, for instance, he knew we'd picked up rumours of inappropriate behaviour in the council chamber. "Whatever would our readers think if we started printing things like that?" The reasoning was apt to puzzle me. Should it be a newspaper's philosophy to print only what Yeovil's stiff-collared, respectable reading public wished to see? Hadn't I, in my idealistic moments, readily swallowed all that noble guff about a free press refusing to pander to anyone (including the influential advertisers)? The weekly paper I worked for had abundant virtues, but its knowledge of reader psychology in those days was still painfully restricted. Of course the readers liked scandal. That was why worthy papers like *The Times* and the *Telegraph* also in time chose not to ignore it.

As a freelance I covered lengthy court cases brimming with sexual content. Tales of satyric clerics on their wayward jaunts away from the pulpit steps or of MPs caught in gay bars were hungrily demanded. Some 'cruisers' lived dangerously and wriggled free of pending publicity. Not that the late MP Tom Driberg bothered too much about the voluminous gossip directed against him. There was a political conference coming up at Weston-super-Mare and Driberg's proclivities were well known. The local constabulary were told to give the various public conveniences a discreet miss as they went about their rounds. He was disarmingly frank about his homosexuality but still needed friends in high places to camouflage his promiscuous sorties. Lord Beaverbrook, his friend when he edited with a mischievous and perceptive pen the William Hickey diary on the *Daily Express*, once persuaded the other Fleet Street barons to suppress an account of Driberg's court appearance. The socialist MP admitted later he was left uneasy about that kind of privilege. It conflicted with the set of political principles that he professed to follow.

It has always appeared to me that anyone who piously rejects the spice of scandal lacks an engrossing measure of intrigue and colour in human nature. That is why, a trifle intrusively, I chuckled when I discovered that Professor Joad, a philosopher of *Brains Trust* fame, was caught cheating and not paying his railway fare at Yeovil Junction; why, attending court one morning in Bristol where a slatternly grey-haired woman of dire misery was fined five shillings for soliciting, I was saddened when an usher confided the wretched defendant was the estranged wife of a famous Arsenal footballer; why I pondered, as I climbed a Nailsworth hill and knocked the door hoping in vain to learn why the late occupant, WH Davies, the *Supertramp* poet, had befriended and married a prostitute before living in that cottage.

I suppose it was an East Coker farmer, Joey Whetham, too well dressed for the hedging and ditching that went with the job, who first of all whetted my appetite for scandalous deeds. He was happier reading about local history and chronicling the incidents that his ancestors passed on than helping with the haymaking. He was an intelligent man, not easily fooled by romantic or blood-curdling extravagances. "But it was true, David. My father used to know the dead man's dad." It surely couldn't be any more authentic than that.

Joey farmed at Pendomer, a hamlet on the extreme edge of East Coker, for more than forty years. The little huddle of cottages, the farmhouse and the redundant, miniscule church haven't changed much over the decades. Nothing could be much more peaceful, more serene. Yet once it rustled with the movement of covert smugglers. They operated from an improvised cavern of rotten tree trunks, branches and undergrowth in the middle of secluded Penn Wood. It was impossible to see them from the main wagon tracks. Over the years, the local smugglers acquired and built up their store of booty, periodically setting off at night to trade with the villains of neighbouring towns and cities.

It was an age of smuggling. East Coker and Pendomer were well placed for the short, profitable journey to the Dorset coast. They were away from their secret Penn Wood retreat on the day that a woodman working for the estate stumbled on the cavern after noticing some new tracks. He was joyfully confronted by the sight of dozens of kegs of spirits and was unable to resist the unexpected bonus. Mr Whetham's version is that the woodman drank liberally and collapsed on the ground. He was found by one of the returning smugglers and was immediately shot. No parish records remain – only the rumours and the conviction of local men like farmer Whetham to stir my free-ranging imagination. It also prompts a Coker memory of an extraordinary West Country lesbian network. This was no more than a margin note, but it at least allowed me fleeting involvement in what, unknown to me, was a bohemian lifestyle and louche contempt for conventional behaviour.

I have already implied my architectural regard for Coker Court. Famous visitors much enjoyed their invitations. Two prime ministers, Asquith and Lloyd George, came to stay for a few days, reflecting maybe a softening Liberal attitude after years of landowning Tory dominance.

Dorothy Heneage was an intelligent and generous hostess. She was delighted that Harold Nicholson and Vita Sackville West spent the first night of their honeymoon at the Court. Other house guests included Osbert Sitwell, the conductor Sir Thomas Beecham and Queen Mary. Mrs Heneage relished the company of the literati of the day. Probably the gossip, too.

In l940 Alice Keppel arrived for a week. She stayed for two years. She'd been, of course, the celebrated mistress of Bertie, Prince of Wales and later King Edward VII. Many saw her as the scarlet woman of her day, though deftly shielded by courtiers. The village didn't really know what was going on; the locals had no idea who this still striking figure was.

Her daughter, Violet Trefusis, followed her to the lovely Hamstone village. It was all so much more quiet than London where the pair had experienced the blitz. But she got restless. She wanted adventure – and preferably with her own sex. Her sham of a marriage had meant little to her. With time on her hands, she now systematically constructed a network of Sapphic liaisons. From her apparently too boring temporary home in Somerset, she pursued a succession of lovers. One impassioned alliance had been with Pat Dansey who lived with an elderly uncle at Berkeley Castle, in Gloucestershire. There was also the affair with the well-known American socialite, Princesse de Polignac, a subject for muffled hilarity.

Violet didn't mind shocking. She went in for cross-dressing. She flaunted her ambiguities. That was why she was always talked about, why the books about her are still a source of literary frisson.

Simon Heneage, Dorothy's grandson, was able to study mother and daughter at close quarters. "Mrs Keppel was something of a grande dame, with an overpowering personality. I found Violet pretentious. She wasn't a classic beauty by any means, though she had a foreign sexiness about her. And she was a terrible snob."

I met her only once as far as I am aware. The Heneage family and their guests mounted an ambitious production of RC Sherriff's anti-war play, *Journey's End*, at Coker Court for their relatives, school parents and friends. The producer found himself one short and, at some risk for the intimate company, I was summoned to play Private Mason. The part called for no great acting prowess, while my plebeian accent, lacking the public school refinement of the rest of the cast, slotted in adequately. In the finest tradition of Shaftesbury Avenue, I went on with a minimum of rehearsal and an amateur's surfeit of trench-grime make-up.

The play was quite a triumph, the applause prolonged in recognition of much filial affection. Afterwards we were introduced to the VIPs in that responsive audience of two dozen. I can't remember what Violet Trefusis said to me. Only several years later, when I was a cub reporter and vaguely aware of her reputation as 'a social butterfly' with unconventional tastes, did I see my momentary thespian meeting with her as a professionally wasted opportunity.

As an energetic young journalist, not prepared simply to accept the task of recording small-town drabness and conformity, I found sport riddled with scandal. I was kept well informed by mates in the Bristol Rovers side of the way fixed odds betting was eroding the game. At the time of the bribery scandals of 1963, I learned of the players' tea-room meetings and the decision to approach the manager, Bert Tann, a church sidesman and man of old-fashioned principles. He could have quickly sold the two offenders, goalkeeper Esmond Million and striker Keith Williams, in a crafty attempt to recoup the money invested in the two players. Instead, shocked and wanting at first to disbelieve the outrage involving a match at Bradford Park Avenue where it was claimed the two players were ready to fix the result, not in Rovers' favour, Tann made an instant judgement. He suspended the pair and they never played in this country again. There was an ugly climate of match-fixing allegations at the time. The felons, some of them well known in the upper reaches of the game, went to prison, were heavily fined or withdrew in disgrace from the sport which had brought them a living.

Cricket had its scandals, too. There was the time when Ian Botham was the subject of dope allegations. The *Mail on Sunday*, who had a particular interest, legal and financial in the saga, as well as Beefy's gleefully reported physical encounter with suspect bedroom furniture in the West Indies, seemed to think I might be privy to the private life of both Botham and his soul-mate Richards. They went to the trouble of sending down a canny, experienced, sexy Fleet Street campaigner to search for added clues and maybe inveigle me into a few confidential asides. They knew I got on well with IVA and had collaborated with him on his autobiography. As I remember it, she said we might be able to have a more fruitful chat over dinner.

Our hushed conversation in the press box at Taunton provided her with no information. It did take on a slightly more desperate inquisitional tone as some of the answers she needed remained as elusive as ever.

"Does Viv like the occasional joint?"

"Not as far as I know."

"Well, why do they call him Smokey?" She gave up on me and with an eloquent expression of frustration she left the box. Soon we were reading that the *Mail on Sunday* and Botham's advisors had come to an agreement.

One sporting scandal that was never resolved concerned Albert Trott, who played cricket for both Australia and this country and must surely be listed among the game's greatest all-rounders. I only wish I'd seen him play and clout uniquely his historic six off Monty Noble over the pavilion at Lord's. In fact, so many questions remain unanswered. Why was he left out of his national side for the tour party here in 1896? His brother, Harry, was the captain after all. Why was he snubbed by the Aussie authorities, if not his fellow players who liked his convivial ways? Whatever the extent of the cricketing politics and personal relationships, he packed his suitcase in a fit of pique and sailed for England. He qualified for Middlesex and appeared in 223 matches for them.

This is not the place to ruminate on his instinctive brilliance with ball – all ten wickets against Somerset – with bat and immense muscle, causing so many county players to despair. With his statistical feats came tragedy. The day before the start of the 1914-18 war, he shot himself. His money was gone, apart from the four crumpled pound notes he left in his dingy flat, along with a wormy wardrobe, for his landlady. His face had been unhealthily puffed and haggard for weeks. The one-room home was littered with empty beer bottles. He walked with difficulty because of dropsy. The inscription on the simple coffin revealed he was 41. A great and ever-complicated sportsman was given no more than one-line obituaries in the next day's papers; the nation had more catastrophic matters on its mind.

As a journalist I tried in vain to learn more of his eventually wasted life. Apart from the daily record of his cricket, there was little to be gleaned. He talked and joked willingly in the professionals' dressing room about the game and its characters. But there remained a mystifying aura about him. He said virtually nothing about his own private life. The other players suspected he liked women and was not too fussy about their morals. His liaison with a flighty young woman from Taunton was a guaranteed talking point when Middlesex were on a West Country tour. Yet he determinedly kept his team-mates in the dark. He regularly visited her (and, some insisted, paid for her services). When I first covered county cricket, more than sixty years ago, two elderly Somerset supporters, not the kind even mildly given to unsubstantiated rumour and sensation, told me of Albert Trott's dalliances in the market town. They had no doubts and they related their memories with an air of credence.

They are now long dead and, of course, I wish I had extended our chat. Their version – and it is roughly the same as one I heard from others back in the 1950s – was that the young woman who shared a bed at times with Trott was murdered. The police investigation dragged on and apparently the once famous cricketer with appearances for two countries was among those questioned though not suspected in any way. It's a compelling, seedy story, touched by authenticity. There are, I understand, some moves to explore more fully and then publish a biography of the remarkable Alberto. I hope the writer meets with more success than I did.

I missed police questioning, only just, at the time of a contract killing in the village of Yatton in north Somerset. The victim was a keen cricket fan, her husband the county treasurer. My wife and I had been friends and were invited to a party at their home. Several of the Somerset players were also there.

The murder, associated with family intrigue, infidelity and one or two unpleasant women on the free-loving fringes, no more than nominally connected with county cricket, was a story that ran for weeks. One villager came up to me during the inquiries and said, half jokingly: "I suppose you know you're among the suspects." Apparently the police had taken a particular interest in a set of pictures taken at that party to which we were invited. They intended following up, my informant said, by visiting those whose photographs were already framed and in position. We should have been flattered. But the gregarious wife who took the pictures was already dead.

Before I leave the subject of scandal, and my own newspaperman's arguably over-exuberant weakness for these human whims and miscalculations, I re-assert my belief that the most riveting episodes belong unquestionably to Victorian England. The social hypocrisy of the times and the sensual flaws of the wealthy only add to the impact. There have been few more gruesome or memorable killings than those of Jack the Ripper but from the moment I first read of Montague Druitt's inclusion on the interminable list of suspects, I was ensnared. Of course any evidence against him was much too flimsy and he surely had no obvious reason to drown himself in the Thames. But I continue to think of him in his pure white flannels, starring in club cricket during the sunny summer tours, his mind more set on spotting the blacksmith's googly than contemplating with dispassion the defenceless innards of a habitually listless, hungry Whitechapel street girl.

Victorian England rustled seductively behind the curtains of respectability. All those decadent clubs, with their fine addresses, whispered passwords and hedonistic diversions, are hard to equal when it comes to scandalous conduct.

This brings me finally to the Beauforts. I used to be asked from time to time to interview the 9th Duke at Badminton House. He was tall, erect, polite, although there was a permanent intimidating edge to him when, in a taciturn style, he gave his answers in a voice which really belonged to the hunting field with an order, from two furlongs away, to remember to shut the five-bar gate. That was where he was happiest, jumping the fences and taking falls when such exertions were made for younger men. The villagers, estate workers and visiting county players who turned out for his charity matches at Badminton called him 'Master'. He liked a measure of subservience and strongly disapproved of any whiff of scandal around the yard or the kennels.

One of my commissions was to write a series 'Scandals in the West' (I don't appear to have ever been able to get away from salacious matters). Lord Arthur Somerset, the third son of the 8th Duke, was a major in the Royal Horse Guards. As a soldier he was wounded and decorated. His military chums called him 'Podge'. He, too, enjoyed hunting around the folds of the Cotswolds. As to his quiet bachelor life, not too much was known, even by the family.

But in 1889 he was exposed as a central figure in the notorious male-brothel scandal of Cleveland Street. Its titillating details dominated every newspaper. For Lord Arthur it was public disgrace. His cronies did their best for him but any efforts at an establishment cover-up failed abysmally. The recurrent question in every London club and the local Meets was "What's going to happen to Podge?"

He took advice from lawyers and scarpered. A distraught aristocrat on the run, he lived in nervous exile in Budapest, Vienna and Paris. He never came back to England.

The next time I was sent to see the 9th Duke, he gave me a long, icy stare. He'd seen my account of what went on at 19 Cleveland Street, not far from Tottenham Court Road and he shared in the family sense of shame at a time when homosexuality was, of course, illegal.

"Did you need to drag all that up again? Podge could have done without that." It was a short interview. For not the only time in my working life, I felt uneasy.

12

REFLECTIONS

Now comes the time for me to reflect – on the village I left in 1955 but never lost.

East Coker did so much to shape me. Its pastoral calm enfolded and nurtured me in those tender years of the 1930s. I still lie awake at night, remembering the timeless cottages and the sight of weary, uneducated, sweet-natured old men, bending their arthritic backs over the garden gate to gossip to a neighbour.

It was my spiritual base. In Verandah Cottage I was born. From here I went to school and later cycled in search of my first proper job. This was my felicitous home, over the little stream bridge and back beyond the laburnum and hollyhocks that framed the front path.

There was the whiff of cider apples and weather-beaten dung in the air. I loved to see the old-style hayricks, the carters on their rounds, still hot bread delivered off the horse-drawn vans. At this distance it may all sound incorrigibly romantic and sentimental, but once it had a wonderful sincerity about it. Village life today may have attracted owners with two or three cars on the gravel drive, lavatories that flush and newcomers who jarringly use non-rural phraseology. But they have disingenuously changed the pattern.

In defiant cussedness, unrealistic as it may be, I don't want too much change. When I return to East Coker now, I want to hear the chimes ringing out their traditional greetings every three hours, just as they did when my father – with some help from me – wound them and the clock for sixty years. I'd like to see the trio of Hughes brothers again, mending their snares and nets and whistling away as they used to, before heading off for a day's rabbiting. Their feats and specialist skills should have earned them a mention in the *Guinness Book of Records*. I remember writing of their commission to clear the minute Channel Island of Hurn soon after the war. The island was overrun by rabbits: less so after the brothers' visit. They cleared nearly 600 a day and one trusts it was done humanely.

Badgers, as a source of food, were, until fairly recently, still on the menu in parts of Spain, Croatia and China. That reminds me of the one or two Badger Feasts organised at East Coker's village pub. No-one seemed too certain how the badgers were acquired and, amid some controversy, the experimental dish and communal celebrations were discontinued.

My affection for East Coker, at least in its less sophisticated days, stems largely from my admission I suppose that I am a definitive Luddite. New technology mystifies and frightens me. During one spell of employment with the BBC, when VHF was being cautiously introduced, I found myself preparing and reading the early-morning news bulletins for a regional audience. Twice, and I recount it here with no pride, I put the station off the air. Someone thought it was a wise policy for me to be in personal charge of the costly equipment and 'to drive the programme' myself. I have no idea what went wrong. But music had to be played instead of the five-minute bulletin.

One of the engineers had to be summoned at some speed to rectify the embarrassing mishap. A fortnight later, I compounded my dithering inadequacy by again putting the station off the air. After that I discovered I was less frequently on the early-morning shift. But my problems in attempting to read instructions on my various pieces of recording equipment did nothing to improve my appalling reputation. There were at least half a dozen occasions when alone in some improvised studio – one, not far from Swindon Town's ground, that seemed like a broom cupboard – I failed to make contact with the programme to which I was contributing. If only one of my grandchildren, then aged five or six, had been around. I fail to understand how they acquire such sanguine and intuitive skills when it comes to new technical instruments.

I have nervously progressed to a computer which goes wrong on a weekly basis. My two adult children, in-laws and six grandchildren have all been enlisted to put me right. The simple fact is that I am happier using my battered typewriter, even though it is falling apart. I know where to find the keys and I don't have to go on buying new cartridges.

Are there others who yearn for a simple life? At East Coker we once had a clergyman, Charles Powell, who took charge of St Michael's for 44 years. He was a gentle, learned man with a refreshingly broad approach. He had a weakness for quoting the classics, although he also kept an enthusiastic eye on the village's football club. The vicar came to East Coker in 1877 and that was where he stayed, changing little but being on hand to visit the sick or take services, until 1921. The parish didn't welcome too many new ideas. Some of the regulars didn't quite know what to make of Ivor Sanders, a well-intentioned intellectual who administered through the forties and seemed to drift towards an Anglo-Catholic approach. He introduced incense and other High Church traits.

As choirboys, we took it in turn to swing the incense. I'm afraid we lacked reverence. Our aim was to work up a plentiful smoke-screen in advance and then, with an air of innocence, to have the priest in an advanced state of asphyxia as the fug disappeared up his nostrils. The pro-Rome TS Eliot would have been horrified. Nor was Mr Sanders too pleased. Maybe the exuberant, misplaced prank was granted some mitigation when the vicar allowed us to play rounders on his lawn after every choir practice.

Ecclesiastical liberties apart, East Coker was a law-abiding community. We had a village policeman who did his rounds on a bicycle. Most of the boys were afraid of him. My preoccupation with things mildly unlawful was heightened every time I walked up the church path, either to fill the coke scuttle or to rake the grass for my sexton father. The tombstone grimly recording that Nathaniel Cox was killed in the discharge of his duties (why couldn't they just say he was murdered?) was prominently placed and must have provided a chilling introduction to any visitors. He was bludgeoned to death by poachers after challenging them late at night in 1876. It was a harrowing and bloody business, much written about in all the papers, regional and national. PC Cox was 37. I think I was four when the inscription was first read to me. In the years that followed, I read it myself hundreds of time. I still do. We're back to the world of scandal that worryingly held my attention.

Policemen, especially the local bobby, were different creatures when I was growing up. If I was in the garden and PC Edwards or PC Vowles were approaching on their bike, I edged into the house. It was an attitude difficult to analyse. Again it was an amalgam of fear and respect. I shouldn't have been fearful; I used to play with Mr Edwards' son. They used to say that Mr Vowles, a quiet, lugubrious copper, never pursued a single prosecution in his whole working life. I got bolder as I went tentatively into journalism. One PC from another village not so far from mine had a penchant for pretty young shop girls – or, in fact, any pretty girls. He would come to dances at East Coker village hall, relying on me and occasionally another cub reporter never to blow his cover. From my powers of observation, he rarely went home empty-handed. I'd then see him, probably on the Tuesday, in uniform and with the proper bearing of rectitude, stepping into the box to give evidence against a philanderer. Sometimes he would wink as he passed me in the staid courtroom.

I fell foul of a policeman mate of mine only once. I was cycling home in the early hours when someone shouted to me to stop.

"And where's your rear light, then?"

I wandered to where he was standing in the shadows. It was a policeman in uniform. And to my relief, he was one I knew.

"Hello, Gordon. Not expecting to see you tonight."

The retort was icy and formal to my surprise. He asked me for my full name and told me he'd be reporting me. I assumed it was a bit of a joke. We traded a few more words, convivial on my part, and I wished him good-night. "You're going to have to walk, aren't you? You can't ride without a rear light."

This was getting slightly silly. To soften any tension, I said: "Go on, then. Give me 100 yards and see if you can catch me."

I started my walk home and once I was clear of him, I cycled again. "What the hell is the matter with Gordon at two o'clock in the morning? Why's he in such a bad mood?" I asked myself.

Notice of my court appearance came through the post. It happened I was covering court for the *Gazette* on the day of my summons. When my name was called, I stepped from the press bench. This in itself was a matter of some hilarity among my colleagues. The three magistrates added their mirth. But my PC wasn't laughing. He gave his evidence with poker expression. Then I cringed as he said: "The defendant, your worships, then suggested I should give him 100 yards and see if I could catch him."

That was clearly enough comedy for one morning. Fine: five shillings. "Next case, please."

I still don't know what possessed the young policeman. We never exchanged another word. Sadly, not long after, he committed suicide. I have to wonder what kind of mental turmoil he was going through that night as he stood alone for perhaps an hour in a deserted country lane.

But that was an unusual incident at a time when a word of quiet warning from a policeman was all that was required. It preceded the Panda cars and all the paper work.

To my astonishment my father, who lacked height and a commanding voice, was appointed a special constable during the war. He looked good in his uniform and fingered a highly polished truncheon as if it were a phallic symbol. There were six of them with Billy Richards, one of several farmers and renowned for his potent, rough cider, in charge. Yeovil was encircled by barrage balloons which took to the air whenever the aircraft works were threatened.

Dad did his police work with conscientious zeal, never missed a parade – or I imagine a mug of Billy's best – and as far as I know, was only once pulled out for an urgent call in the middle of the night. It was top secret and the rest of the family and a few friends concluded that a parachuted German airman was on the loose or even that a Fifth Columnist was doing his best to disrupt our morale. I'm not certain that my father was actually told what was involved. Only some months later was it revealed that there had been an attempted rape. Nothing at all to do with national security or a German pilot badly off course. Something of a let-down when Coker's full contingent of 'Specials' were on the case.

This is my 25th book, not a bad statistic in my case. It illustrates a gradual professional shift, although I still insist on describing myself on documents and other bureaucratic waffle as a journalist. I refuse to part company with the job that I have loved, if poorly remunerated, for most of my life. I started, however, with a calculated move into a publishing world I knew nothing about, by experimentally ghosting autobiographies of others who had every reason to bask in a public glow and had a story worth telling. This I found a stimulating exercise – taking over someone else's life for a few weeks, getting inside their heads, extracting their best anecdotes and touching on a few of their indiscretions.

Alan Gibson, at times my mentor, admonished me. "What are you doing – writing someone else's book? For heaven's sake, try writing your own." And indeed that was what I began doing, with varying commercial success.

But ghosting had its merits for me. I didn't limit myself to cricket after having worked in tandem with Viv Richards and Zaheer Abbas, the glorious Pakistan stylist. My book, *Ladies Mile*, for instance, a slim, unusual profile charted in the first person, gave me considerable pleasure and satisfaction, not to mention a tilt at civic pomposity in Bristol. Victoria Hughes' unworldly account of her days as a lavatory attendant on the Downs in Bristol during the Depression years and after was full of refreshing innocence, a quality I have always cherished. She befriended many of the prostitutes, who plied their carnal trade against the tree trunks. They hired out their arid bodies for a pittance. My author, a wholesome, ageing woman who continued to cycle around Bristol's busy streets for her shopping when she was almost eighty, retained an inspiring dignity. Ladies Mile, once renowned as the sylvan side road where wealthy women rode their horses on Sunday mornings before church, was transformed to a scene of whispered bartering after dark. It took Victoria months before she realised why those haggard part-time pros gathered to count the small change in her lavatory. She poured them tea from her pot; she listened mesmerised and at the same time shocked by their coarse language; and she admitted to me just "how excited I got when eventually I discovered what they were doing". It wasn't that she approved of this kind of crude prostitution in the cold night air. But she had stumbled on a segment of the rich city's rough, working-class vice and it was like an entirely new adventure story for her. The fact that they all treated her as a confidante, allowing her to share vicariously their sordid experiences, added to the unpredictable drama that coloured her life. She was a social worker without realising it.

Not only the prostitutes shared Victoria's pot of tea

The council appeared to condemn the book's publication. I don't think it was ever stocked in any of Bristol's many public libraries. One corporation official told me in highly charged, censorious tones: "Not the kind of record we want on display." I can only add that the book, bravely published by Abson Books at the giveaway cover price of £1.20, rapidly sold out.

Victoria died soon after. But she had made her own valuable contribution to Bristol's social history. I trust that a hypocritical city council has accepted that and has kept a copy or two in its comprehensive archives.

When I was writing the modest 67-page book of her extraordinary reminiscences, I would call at her neat Horfield home where we would sip a glass of sherry and talk again about some of the more outrageous and poignantly bedraggled women who lived in constant physical risk as they picked up their ten-shilling notes or often less on the wind-swept Downs for tawdry services rendered. Perhaps attitudes have finally changed. In 2004 a Bristol City Council blue plaque was unveiled above the door of the Stoke Road ladies' toilets commemorating 'Victoria Hughes (1897-1978) who befriended and cared for prostitutes when she worked here from 1929 to 1962.' Could the much-maligned political correctness have had a hand in making amends?

Victoria Hughes never remotely peddled pornography. She kept a diary of the people she met and, with objective precision and no sense of shame, she jotted down her observations in pencil on the pages of a big exercise book. She was a simple social bystander and not once could she have been accused of any judgemental conclusions. It would have been rather grand to suggest that our partnership was literary. It was, however, a lesson for me in conveying without confection a compassionate aspect of the human scene.

I warmed to ghosting, even if the pulp market was inundated with the bogus sentiments of celebrities who had nothing to say and leaned on the invention of their enlisted hack to spray meaningless narrative around the glossy pictures. About this time I could have pursued a part-time career as a professional ghost. Fortunately I had the good sense to remain selective. I wrote lengthy pieces for Tom Jones, and Robin Cousins with whom I had at least an intimate liaison of a sort. He was born in the small maternity ward in Bristol which was also occupied by my wife, awaiting the arrival of her first child. The two boys were delivered by the same staff in a matter of hours.

Ghosting demanded no exceptional skills, although I understand some subjects could be tetchy – maybe for the best of reasons – and felt they needed a revision of literary assistance. That happened with Colin Cowdrey, the cricketer, and Ted Heath, the politician.

Some of these projects were a joy. David Shepherd, the beefy, benign umpire and friend, asked me to help him with his autobiography. He had a good memory, a glowing feel for his native Devon, much natural humour to match his rubicund features, and a close knowledge of famous cricketers and their temperamental flaws. We used to meet at a motorway service station, where I would make copious notes and occasionally delve deeper. That was my one qualification – he hated exploring and revisiting rows and differences. David walked away from anything that was confrontational. Our relationship remained steadfast and I was privileged that he asked me to put the words on paper. But Shep was a happy man and I struggled to edge him, however tactfully, towards the side of cricket that conflicted with the cosy Instow ambience and the estuary water lapping the boundaries of the lovely ground just across the road from his beloved home.

Ghosting held out its bonuses, even when they didn't all materialise. Roddy Bloomfield, most delightful and gregarious of London's publishers, once phoned and asked me if I was in the mood to travel at short notice to the States.

"Who do you want me to see?"

"Elizabeth Taylor."

No bad way to begin a conversation. I immediately lied and said I was free. One of Richard Burton's brothers was ready to go into print, I was told. But it would need someone to guide his steps. It appeared that Elizabeth Taylor was prepared to offer some thoughts on the Celtic clan. The trouble was that several other publishers were aware of the proposed book. Speed was an essential part of the deal. If we were lucky, how soon might I be available to fly to see Miss Taylor?

"Tomorrow," I said with a flamboyant, unconsciously affected Welsh lilt to my voice.

The book came out, but not with the interview that would have meant I'd been engaged for some judicious amplification of Burton childhood. It went, I believe, to another publisher. I went to bed only to dream of the violet-eyed Taylor.

Such experiences gave me a professional lift. I continued to sniff a news story with enthusiasm, deciding in which direction to offer it. On Saturdays I still sent my football or county cricket reports. Too briefly, after the *Sunday Correspondent* was launched, I was given a regular match. Suddenly, when I should probably have been consigned to the reporting of more pedestrian pastimes like bowls, I found myself at Old Trafford, Villa Park, White Hart Lane, Anfield and Highbury – or in the sunshine at Lord's and Trent Bridge. These were the sporting heights that I had assumed were, for me, gone for ever – with only two Cup Finals and a single Test match to show for it. The *Correspondent*, which sadly wouldn't be around for long, allowed me lots of words and, despite the rejected temptations of over-indulgence, I wallowed in the hitherto prohibited acres of rain forest. I was allowed to look beyond the winning goal or Paul Gascoigne's wondrous intuition (though he remained my favourite). For one long cricket match report in, I think, the *Observer*, my car broke down on the motorway and I arrived at the ground, spattered with oil and panic, in mid-afternoon. There was a message waiting for me that an additional first-edition 900-word report was urgently needed in, well … fifteen minutes at the most. Scyld Berry, for years a good friend and conveniently covering the same fixture, detected my plight. He gave me a detailed summary of the day's play to date. There was no time for any comfortable seating or wordy flights; I used a nearby car bonnet and ad-libbed my piece. It read well enough, invested deceptively with commendable authority, although it should have carried a double by-line.

Breakdowns aren't uncommon. That is evident, too, with the wonders of new technology. On the day of Brian Lara's 501 against Durham at Edgbaston, I was saved by my Luddite inclinations. Lara was going on and on, to such an extent that most of cricket's top writers, away at Nottingham covering a Test match, felt they should be in Birmingham. So they headed off to chronicle the little Trinidadian's final overs of consummate triumph. the *Guardian*, often loyal employers in those days, said they were prepared to leave history, if it was about to be made, to me.

I relate what happened as no statement of skill. It was luck and a reliance on antiquated methods. I had no lap-top or technological aids to speed me on my way. What the *Guardian* needed was 900 words for the news pages and the same amount for Sport. It was wanted in some haste at the end of the day's play, along with an interview with Lara. The latter was arranged for all of us by Warwickshire but, as best I recall, Lara was still a comparatively young man without a too articulate or ready turn of phrase. He wasn't at that time the most popular of Edgbaston residents, either.

For a technical reason that eludes me, several of the senior cricket correspondents were having trouble with their varying systems of communication. Expletives were understandably flying about. Edition times were pressing with remorseless indifference to the writers' physical and mental state. I had opted, as I invariably did then, for the ludicrously old-fashioned method of dictating my pieces direct to a proficient copy-taker in the office, whose dependable form of employment was becoming superfluous in the contentious name of progress. But her service suited me. It allowed me the chance to extemporise as I went; to throw an insight into the story as it occurred to me, to reshape an opinion.

We all had long reports to file on Lara's historic innings. And I genuinely think I was first to finish. I left the press box for a beer, retreating from good mates toiling in some cases with an unresponsive system and widespread oaths. 'Bloody progress,' I mused, as I came down the stairs.

I was never really a competitive soul. I liked to share a pint and a story (well, not the juiciest and most eagerly researched ones!). But trying to beat a friend to a solitary phone box, a deadline and a tale of true newsworthiness were always part of the fun. Much of that fun has now gone. Newsrooms and sports desks have become soulless. Once jovial columnists now do much of their work at home, then send it by computer to the sports editors. Supper breaks, for years the civilised outlets for raucous laughter and gossip for desk-bound sub-editors, have gradually disappeared. Reporters look weary-eyed from hours peering against their natures at computer screens. The unpretentious language has changed. Graduates squeeze into journalism with often meaningless degrees. Some, the lucky ones, have benefited from practical tuition; others have no idea what questions to ask or how to break down the turgid defences of a key interviewee. An understanding of human nature and absorbing sense of curiosity have faithfully guided me.

Nearly all the papers now look alike. The similarity of design and shoddy subbing have taken away much of the brio. Journalism, in the provinces and at national level, is rigidly governed by mean budgets and time schedules that at times mock any pretence of immediate news. What happened to the flutter of excitement when evening papers churned out with remarkable efficiency one edition after another? In my days of court reporting, we scribbled a succession of new stories based on the varying cases. Then a messenger boy would arrive to collect them and rush them back to the office. Mike Averis was one well versed in that fleet-footed role. He went on to become a fine journalist himself, like his father before him, and there is some irony in the fact that, years later, he was my sports editor on the *Guardian*.

My daughter Julia, married to BBC TV news presenter and reporter David Garmston, followed me into newspapers before television production. I made no overt effort to influence her but was privately pleased when she also chose journalism for a career. Sadly I find it hard to recommend the job now. The best reporters aren't measured by the number of long words that they use. Too many show off in their columns which they irksomely overload with first-person singular. The first time I collected John Arlott's signature and asked his advice about future work in a newspaper office, he said: "Try not to use 'I'. People don't need to hear your opinion all the time." It was wise counsel that he personally adhered to.

I have often argued that a decent journalist should be an adept bluffer. That isn't meant to imply that I advocate the approach of a charlatan. But the news reporter, for instance, talks to dozens of differing people every week. Many of them are specialists in their subjects. So it is totally unreasonable for the interviewer to be able to share a kindred knowledge in every case. What he owes, however, is an apparent enthusiasm in the matters to be discussed. To demonstrate an embarrassing ignorance in the subject is an insult and counter-productive.

Despite my years covering sport, I knew nothing about tennis; nor did I have much more than a working knowledge of its internal politics or the strangely prickly natures of some of those who played at top global level. I was sent at various times to interview Rod Laver, Doris Hart and Arthur Ashe when they came to play in Bristol. We got along well and they ended up confiding some of the locker-room intimacies that I imagine they would normally only have passed on to a fellow tennis zealot. They assumed I knew and liked the game.

In the same way I was sent to have a few words with Sir Thomas Beecham when he came to conduct an orchestral concert in Bath; and extending the musical spectrum, I was told to bring back profiles of Gracie Fields – and her bloody aspidistra – as well as the endearingly gormless George Formby after topping the Hippodrome bill on his final show. I think that I emerged with passable credit.

One of the early lessons I learned was that I had to be able to take a rebuff; they are dispensed all too eagerly by pompous officials and self-important stage grandees. Frank Maddox, who used to run the Theatre Royal at Bath, had a pathological disaffection for critics. In one contemptuous letter to me, when he'd decided not to send first-night tickets to one of his plays, he wrote: "I don't need you – we've got a full house anyway." As if our obligation was solely to sell his seats when business was sluggish.

It was some kind of badge of honour when we were banned by a football club. Graham Russell, a well-known and outspoken West Country journalist, was refused a ticket to Swindon Town matches for some weeks after one parochial spat with the club about something he'd written. Bristol Rovers' Bert Tann dispensed bans with what seemed like profligate delight when Eastville's writers crossed the expected public relations lines. It usually only lasted for a week or so, by which time his anger had subsided. Then he'd join us for post-match reconciliation. Blissfully at those elongated drinking sessions, we would rarely discuss football. Bert, once a painter and decorator at the Dorchester Hotel in London, was an impassioned socialist. He was an eloquent talker and kept us going with his religion, left-wing persuasions and – remembering the reason for our pleasant bacchic indulgence – forgiveness on his part. At some time in our careers of sports writing, we were all victims of tetchy management. I was on one occasion, after part of a hitched lift in the Bristol City team coach for a journey to an FA Cup game in Yorkshire, put out on a bleak hillside miles from anywhere. The manager, Pat Beasley, a usually mild-mannered chap who talked in monosyllabic blandness, had just been told of a relatively innocuous story

I had written in that day's early-edition *World* back in Bristol. It had been leaked for me by one of my friends in the team.

Pat was untypically outraged. He ordered the driver to stop the coach. "You'll never travel with us again. Now you can find your own way to the ground," he told me in a Stourbridge voice more raised than I had ever heard from him before.

The rebuke was sustained for a quarter of an hour. It was a misty day and for a time I hoped the whole of Yorkshire would be engulfed in a swirling blizzard. But visibility improved and in time I was reprieved. Sheepishly I climbed back on the coach, sitting next to my source, to obscure, I hoped, any tell-tale sign of fractured mateyness. The players stifled amused whispers. And the journey continued. It was my only turbulent exchange with Beasley, a manager held in high esteem because of his pragmatic style on the training ground.

During the seasons I reported and trod the beat of Bristol City and Bristol Rovers, I was permanently mesmerised by the disparity in demeanour between the two clubs. Rovers were the humbler club; their history had been unkind to them. They had survived fires, fog and floods, a Board of Trade inquiry and the bribery scandal of 1963. There was never any money to spare but the loyalty of their fans, however restricted in number, was perhaps unmatched in affectionate feeling.

Their board, apart from skirmishes with a greyhound company faction, didn't interfere in footballing matters. The directors were known as faceless men. The odd photograph which emerged from the docile board meetings made them appear more like the occupants at a Lodge meeting than modestly monied men grateful to be sitting behind their polished boardroom table, while retaining a No Buy-No Sell policy, which meant they could hold on to talented Bristol lads like Geoff Bradford and Alfie Biggs. The secretary, John Gummow, was obsessed by the belief that there was a glaring imbalance in the measure of publicity afforded the two Bristol clubs. More than once, he marched uninvited into the *World* building, clutching a ball of string to make his preoccupied small-minded point. Meticulously he stretched his string on the table as he measured the number of column inches that both clubs had been given over the previous week.

It was a fatuous experiment. George Baker, the sports editor, went to inordinate lengths to ensure that any bias was avoided

By contrast, City's board was an amiable miscellany of extrovert and thirsty directors. Harry Dolman was the powerful, autocratic chairman. His voice carried the clout. He didn't like dissenters. On the days that City won, he'd invite the reporters into the boardroom.

I made sure that I wouldn't get too close to the directors of either club. Ethical questions like that always bothered me a little. In search of a quote from another of the Ashton Gate managers, Peter Doherty, I phoned and put a challenging question to him. Peter got on better with the Press than he did the players. "I'll leave it to you, David. You know the way I think. I can trust you to say what I need to say." It demanded a warm relationship and I didn't ever abuse it. Not that I would ever have taken a similar liberty with Bert Tann.

One of my toughest moral dilemmas came in more recent years when I was writing my biography of Wally Hammond. I had suppressed certain facts about his private life for a long time. My sources were unimpeachable and after some torment I put into print details of his medical condition. It was not shocking any more in the 1990s and I felt it largely accounted for his moodiness, lending as it did a greater understanding for his surly and less attractive personality traits.

In a very different context, there was one other incident that left me uneasy. In my Yeovil days, one of the essential weekly calls for parish church information was passed on to us by a shy, helpful assistant priest. All the reporters got on well with him; he wasn't at all stuffy and we would on occasions share a coffee with him. He laughed at the innocent stories we told of our girl friends. There was nothing obviously perverse or spooky about him.

Then, covering the court one Friday morning, we were all surprised when his name was called and he was brought up from the cells. He was more wan than usual. He wasn't wearing his normal dog collar and he looked in need of a shave. The assistant priest was up on a sexual charge. I don't even remember the details now, but what I do remember was his face of anguish as he looked towards the press box and saw us all there. We exchanged glances and then looked down. There was tangible guilt from both sides. At this distance I don't recall what happened to him, although I think he was possibly remanded in custody. Very soon I was off to do my National Service, and I never discovered whether he returned to his church duties. We only added to his shame, reporting as we did the token couple of paragraphs in all the local papers, listing amid the fidgety innuendos his name and alleged offence.

Away from journalistic aspirations and such matters of the conscience as the erring trainee priest, I wondered at times what other creative scope was open to me. Back in my National Service days, my attention had been aroused when I heard that a group of technicians were planning a variety show for RAF Thorney Island. One of them was Dudley Sutton, later to become a familiar face as a character actor on television. I asked if I could join them and said I would let them see one or two of my sketches. My enthusiasm was for a few days unlimited – I borrowed a typewriter from one of the offices, and to Sutton and his intended concert party I submitted not just one or two sketches but virtually a complete show. I included ideas from my East Coker thespian jaunts and some topical jokes about navigational schools, just like the one where I'd been seeing out my closing months of so-called patriotic enlistment. The variety show concept, alas, died an early death. Several of the entertainers were posted. So were my scripts – I never saw them again.

Alongside my journalism was an unformulated ambition to turn myself into a comedy writer. I landed two pieces on *Braden's Week* and two more, brief and without dialogue, for a late night TV revue show based in Bristol, *Whatever Next*. The going rate seemed to be £46 an item. During a few months at TWW, forerunner of HTV, I was encouraged to do a wedding-day skit for Stan Stennett. Unfortunately the likeable Stan forgot his words and a few decent one-liners were lost.

But I quietly thought there might be a new part-time career for me. Michael Palin, not long out of university and taking his first tentative steps in television, was doing some comedy in a half-hour show for TWW, in the days when regional companies were being invited to originate ideas. The small group, with their virgin Equity cards, used to drink at a decrepit little pub on the Bath Road, between the end of rehearsals and transmission. I went along, too, as a bit of an intruder. I didn't know Palin (still don't) but he struck me as a thoroughly nice bloke. The show didn't last for long and I could see it needed a more expansive budget.

On an impulse several years later, I wrote to Michael Palin, via his agent, and submitted some ideas for no particular slot. His reply came quickly and, with more significance, helpfully. He wrote six pages in his own handwriting. He told me the sketches that he didn't think would work – and why. And he particularly liked one running gag. He suggested how it could still be developed. There was no indifference or impatience. He had no show of his imminently on the stocks, of the kind that might be right for my approach, but he hoped it might be possible to explore the idea of mine that he clearly liked.

More or less at the same time, I was hired for a day to assist the playwright Alan Melville, who was acting as the presenter for a bid in Bristol to launch a new commercial radio station, He, too, was marvellously encouraging when I admitted that I was really getting nowhere with my TV sketch-writing aspirations.

He began by telling me who to avoid if I wanted to send sketches and script ideas to performers. The list was a surprisingly long one, suggesting that plagiarising was as rife in light entertainment as in the shadowy corners of publishing. With show business and so many offshoots, I decided it was usually impossible to cite the offender and assemble the evidence. And was it vaguely worth the time and expense?

I made a note of Alan Melville's warning of light-fingered sketch-writers. His most perspicacious advice came when he said: "Latch onto an emerging comic. He's going to be the one looking for new material."

That evening I studied the notice of what was coming soon to the Bristol Hippodrome. Someone called Mike Yarwood was my first candidate. But did impressionists need gags? He apparently didn't; there was no reply to my letter.

An off-beat comedian, Freddie Davies, on his way to the Hippodome the following week, was my next recipient. He had odd-style lips that he puckererd incessantly and he wore a bowler. He called himself Mr Parrotface. I'd seen him a few times on television and thought he had an original line in comedy. But the scope he allowed himself was restricted – he would soon need a new direction. A letter from me was waiting for him when he appeared at the Hippodrome on the following Monday. On the Tuesday he phoned me.

Yes, he liked everything I had suggested, especially the new-style children's show. Would I let him have a format straightaway? And – hold on a minute – might I consider packing in my present job, whatever it was, and join him full-time to see how successfully we could work together? That was sweeping stuff, tempting too. But I already knew a little about the pitfalls of show business. My genes, nurtured from generations of canny men on the Somerset-Dorset border, guided me. I thanked Freddie, stalled and, with a few misgivings, put my comedy writing finally to rest.

I like to think there was some comedy in a semi-autobiographical book, *Country Reporter*, that I wrote and which went into paperback. The idea came from an influential and ever-helpful publisher, Graham Tarrant, who saw it as a possible TV series. For that reason I planned my authentic adventures episodically. Reaction was more effusive than I had dared to hope. The BBC took out an option.

"You could be earning real money for the first time. But it's a different world, full of frustrations. For a start you need an agent," I was told.

An agent? Now yes, it really was different. With kindly encouragement, Paul Vaughan took me on. He'd shown his selective skills by having Larry Grayson and Chris Tarrant on his books. I must have been a bit of a time-consuming let-down and risk. But the ritual process towards a TV series moved, at least theoretically, into brisk action. The agent approved of the visual way I had created my tales, building them around a cast list of characters plucked from my provincial newsroom.

Progress, it seemed to me, was being made with indecent haste. The senior BBC drama producer, Barry Hanson, had no personal wish to let go. Keith Waterhouse, whose early years in journalism were similar to mine, was commissioned to provide four sample episodes, directly based on my book and fashioned for television. I was taken grandly to the Ivy to discuss the project over a meal. As we talked, I spotted another diner taking a repeated look at me from behind a draped curtain. I mentioned this to Waterhouse. "Oh, that's only my chum Ned Sherrin. I told him about the possible series and that you both came from rural Somerset. He's just sussing you out." Now they are both dead; my book and Keith's scripts live on, after a fashion. I don't know what happened, but I understand that TV's drama routes are littered with false hopes. Apparently my conscientious agent has no wish to let go.

I draw to a close. My inner thoughts still don't stray far from East Coker. Nor do my books. Death duties and taxation brought a brutal closure to the Court estate which for a long, formative time moulded me. Once, in my silent, increasingly sceptical days towards adulthood, I looked down from the top of the church tower and wished for a fairer, more egalitarian distribution of the parish's wealth and ownership. Then I saw much of that opulence clawed away by perhaps overdue changes. My Verandah Cottage was the last timeless property in the village to be sold; that to me represents loyalty and good intent by the Heneage family.

Loyalty, like moral courage, is a specific quality of the countryman. I can recall, on that theme, nothing more inestimably touching than the gesture of farewell that local farmer Peter Mead chose for his prize-winning Dorset Horn sheep. The Mead family had farmed in East Coker for several generations. Peter was proud of his sheep. He lambed them, cared for them, led them into the prize ring. And when he knew he was dying, he arranged for them to be around for the funeral service. His coffin was borne on a trailer and pulled by a tractor. The sheep, which had been his life, bunched in seeming repose in a corner of the paddock, nearest to the church. At Peter's request, the cortège paused for a moment or two before continuing its ascent the short distance to St Michael's.

Peter Mead's sheep

Perhaps I shall be allowed to end with a personal story that remains as confusing and far-fetched as it is hilarious and fantastical. I bracket it with a slightly shamefaced confession that my overall regard for academia has never been as high as it should be. It comes, I suppose, from my own deficient depths of proper scholarship and a loitering feeling of inferiority, often there though seldom bothering me.

Now is the moment to reveal that my name is Tom Stoppard. Or, to put it another way, his name is David Foot.

Explanation is surely demanded, and it goes back to the 1990s when I received a letter from a lecturer in English at Bath College. With commendable restraint, he told me that a book had just arrived from America, written by a Professor Katherine Kelly, of Texas University, who informed the reader in pretty unambiguous terms that in the late 1950s, our own and treasured Tom Stoppard had been operating as a journalist under the name of David Foot.

Professor Kelly clearly went into more detailed research than that. In her book she says that her subject spent four years on the *Western Daily Press* in Bristol "probably using the initials DDF shortly before resigning to join the *Evening World* with now the full-blown pseudonym David Foot." This account must seem to be turning into an unmitigated exercise in egotism, for which I can only offer my apologies. But the professor's biography, *Tom Stoppard and the Craft of Comedy* (it's that, all right) becomes even more extraordinary with its theories. It gets its facts right about Bristol's morning paper but DDF, for instance, was another contemporary journalist in the office, Durban Frost, later to become a versatile BBC radio correspondent.

I can only quote the American author directly. "Sometime during 1959, Stoppard's own name began to appear under some theatre reviews, other reviews as well as soccer columns were signed David Foot … the name David Foot may have been Stoppard's parody of 'William Boot', the bumbling reporter in Evelyn Waugh's novel *Scoop*."

And on it goes: ingenious, rather clever, amusing (unless you are the real Stoppard) and remarkably inaccurate. I did work on the *World* at the same time as him, helping him out with his Pitman's when his concentration was lapsing and bounding instead in a dozen different directions of imagination at our regular Friday morning police court commitments when we were working for rival papers.

It was, by any standards, an appalling piece of research – even though it doubtless retains its place on university library shelves in the States. Tom was told of the shoddy biographical portrait and wisely ignored it. As I said at the time, with impish optimism, I should perhaps approach Stoppard in search of overdue royalties and follow with a cheeky request to know whether Rosencrantz and Guildenstern's Boswell has over the years been surreptitiously trading on my name.

I don't think I have ever taken myself too seriously, by trying to set social or intellectual targets that haven't come naturally and would have threatened to lead me off the well-trod rural tracks that enthralled and guided me through my wide-eyed boyhood. My instinct and boyhood have served me well – as have the long lines of oaks that my family first planted generations ago. The trees are as ageless as the parish and Verandah Cottage. My footsteps down the road have been an enthralling adventure.

Julia, Mark, Anne and David

A MISCELLANY OF WRITING

DAVID SHEPHERD – AN OBITUARY

Guardian, 2009

David Shepherd, who has died of cancer aged 68, was one of the best and most respected cricket umpires in the world, his good nature bolstered by native Devonian wisdom. He umpired 92 Tests and 172 one-day internationals, progressing to the elite panel, while earning widespread, non-partisan praise for his tact, judgement and integrity in a game too easily distracted by irritatingly volatile performers. Rosy-cheeked, distinctively Falstaffian, with the girth of someone who liked food and warm-hearted company, 'Shep' was one of the most familiar white-coated figures on the global cricket circuit.

His duties took him to all the most famous grounds. He found himself staying in exotic hotels and was at times feted by dignitaries of the host nations. Yet he was happiest of all strolling on the sand dunes near his Devon estuary home at Instow with Jenny, his partner, and Skip the dog. He lived only a few boundary lengths away from the lovely North Devon Cricket Club ground where, as a boy, he had first watched games while chasing the rabbits off the outfield, and where he later played in front of the thatched pavilion.

Shep was a nervous man, whether waiting his turn to bat for Gloucestershire or going to bed early on the eve of a Test match featuring illustrious and often contentious players. He hated confrontation, preferring to convey a rebuke with a discreet, if still unequivocal, word to the felon at the end of the over. Some of his umpiring took place during the largely pre-technology age. His self-imposed philosophy encouraged the practice of a two-man partnership. He used to say: "In a difficult moment, I would look at the other umpire. All that was needed was a reassuring glance and nod from one to the other."

He might have looked fat and jovial, but he was never a show-off. There were, though, his renowned idiosyncratic motions, accompanied by those quaint balletic hops whenever the scoreboard registered a Nelson – the number 111 – or one of its multiples. That always guaranteed guffaws, and a Brian Johnston-style moment or two of whimsy in the commentary box. It also endeared him to those whose knowledge of the game was minimal. Shep, when asked for an explanation for his antics, would hazily put them down to superstition, or the effects of obscure Devon myth and legend. As with many diffident people, he quite enjoyed the dramatic demands of such rituals. The cameras would zoom in to catch his half-smile.

Born in Bideford, Devon, Shep was in every sense a village boy and retained an unworldly charm. His father, a useful club cricketer and rugby full-back who once played in a Welsh trial, was a chief engineer in the Merchant Navy. His mother, hard-working and assertive, was a big influence on his life. For years she ran the local post office, a position of some standing and a social focal point. Shep's brother, Bill, in turn took it over while Shep helped with the paper round. Bill was also a gifted cricketer who spent three years being coached at Lord's and captained the MCC Young Professionals. He was, in Shep's view, the better player, but he chose to stay at the post office, limiting his all-round talents to the Minor Counties Cricket Association and club matches.

Shep went to Barnstaple Grammar School and ended up as head boy. He was in the school XI for six years and, in his final season, topped 1,000 runs. Rugby held at bay his tendency to put on weight. He played at scrum-half for South Molton, a convivial club that wore a slightly intimidating all-black strip. But sport was still only a weekend obsession. His parents were more mindful of the future, and he was guided to St Luke's College, Exeter, with the intention that he would become a teacher, which he did – for a short time.

His cricket reputation was growing. There were big scores for Devon in the Minor Counties and hundreds for North Devon and his college. Those who watched him liked the manner in which he belted the ball off the front foot. He went to Kent for a trial but in 1965 joined Gloucestershire at an annual salary of £500. His first-class debut was at the Parks against Oxford. He chain-smoked as he waited his turn to bat – and then scored a century. The experienced pros he played alongside exchanged nods of approval.

Shep went on to make 282 appearances for the county, twice exceeding 1,000 runs in a season. But he was at times not sure of a place in the side. He was told, at first with a kindly grin and then more sternly, that he was carrying too much weight. He did not warm to the strictures that went with his onerous training schedule. On one cross-country run, when he usually brought up the rear, he was caught out by his captain and team-mates who were hiding in a bush as he sheepishly went past them in a milk float.

Humour was never far away. He was mischievously ever ready to relate tales of those celebratory evenings when, inexplicably, he lost both his car and his shoes. The umpires on the county circuit and those of higher international rankings liked him, too. They approved of the way he dealt with blustering troublemakers at the crease. They were aware how much he detested batsmen, some famous, who affected an air of innocence when they knew well enough that they had got a touch.

But even the finest of umpires make mistakes. He always owned up and later in the match might have a confidential chat with the batsman he had ruled out leg before.

His nadir came at Old Trafford in 2001, England against Pakistan, when he failed to detect three no-balls with which Saqlain Mushtaq took wickets. He was mortified and at the same time puzzled that no warning was conveyed to him by walkie-talkie. Shep hurried away from the ground, near to despair.

167

He decided on the spot to end his career as a top umpire, and only the daily phone calls from friends, Lord's, players and umpires persuaded him to change his mind.

For most of the time, however, his gentle cream-tea voice engendered chuckles and above all, respect. He had been a first-class umpire since 1981, making his Test debut four years later. His final Test was at Kingston in 2005. He was embarrassed by the volume of acclaim that came his way with retirement. But he knew how much he was going to miss it all. Sitting in an armchair, watching international cricket on the box, was not the same.

Shep suffered from diabetes, and then drastic weight loss and cancer. He is survived by Jenny, whom he married last year.

Shep serving in the Instow post office

BACALL OF DUTY WAS A DOUBLE DELIGHT

Guardian, 2009

Sportsmen have always tended to hunt and excel in pairs. Whatever their individual talents, we remember them especially in duplicate. It was Larwood and Voce, Hobbs and Sutcliffe, Trueman and Statham, Thomson and Lillee.

But Gow and Bacall? Er, that needs a little explanation. This, I suppose, is where pairings veer from the more obvious. We accept that fast bowlers, predacious by nature, like to prowl in twosome pursuit of a kill. Opening batsmen, attuned to each other's whims and insecurities, benefit from the unspoken assurances from a familiar mate down the track. It isn't just cricket, of course. Rugby has its muscled and menacing props who not only go round together but look, with their scowls and shaven heads, uncannily alike.

In my more youthful and active journalistic days I worked best with conflicting simultaneous briefs. These involved theatre and sport. The only complication was the logistical one when I had to make the challenging choice between Gielgud declaiming or Charlie George screaming for the ball.

Last week I came across a torn and faded newspaper cutting of an eventful meeting I had in February 1979. It was with Lauren Bacall so, sentimentally at least, it was worth keeping. She was in this country to publicise her autobiography and was in a bad mood. She didn't much like journalists and, no doubt because she had left her make-up case behind in London, she was less than welcoming to half a dozen photographers and TV cameramen who had also turned up at the bookshop in Bristol.

As I arrived, weary from lugging a heavy Uher radio tape-recorder up a long hill, she was leaving. It was an unscheduled early exit. The engine of her swish limo was already purring and her step on to the pavement was as purposeful as that of any Ashton Gate striker. For one impecunious freelance, her face of thunder spelled financial disaster and panic. My presumptuous intentions counted for nothing.

If this sounds like shameless name-dropping, I apologise. But I shall eventually get to the point of this Friday-morning episode involving the style, ageless allure and histrionic range of the actress who once melted Bogart enough to become his wife. It was no time now for rerunning scenes from *Key Largo* or *The Big Sleep*, which I had studiously researched in preparation. Instead, for one of the few times in a diverse professional life, I let my instincts take over. I jumped in beside the driver and, as if wholly dispassionate about what was happening, I directed him to a small fish restaurant a mile away. My instructions had come out with affected authority. In the back of the limo, La Bacall was spluttering her protests; a young PR woman, equally puzzled, was doing her best to placate her.

There is not a word of exaggeration in this account. The driver clearly thought I was part of the retinue. He pulled up at the restaurant and Bacall, flustered and still confused, followed us in. She rejected and then accepted a double gin, and I ordered a Dover sole for her. Blissfully, her rant at the expense of the Fourth Estate gradually subsided. Perhaps she really was, after all, 'this nice Jewish girl who had been plucked for stardom', as the book blurb told us. I got my lengthy, cooperative radio interview and enough anecdotes for a newspaper piece next morning.

By then we were on more confidential terms. "The trouble is I've got so many things on my mind – like driving back to London and catching my plane at Heathrow," she said. "I know the feeling," I replied with intimate candour. "I have to see Gerry Gow, you know. Yes, another interview." I might as well have said Stanislavsky by the silence my words created.

The revelation made no apparent impact. She must surely have heard of Gerry. Everyone in the West Country had. But I let it pass. He was now top of my agenda, this tousle-haired Glaswegian veteran of 300-plus games for Bristol City who most Saturdays left scarlet stud marks as a ritualistic parting present to his opponents. He didn't believe in fannying about in midfield. He instilled fear: plenty of raw drama there. It is unlikely Gow ever went to a Bristol Old Vic matinée on a free afternoon.

I've no idea whether Gow would be flattered to be bracketed with Bacall. Yet the two of them remain affectionately wedged, at least psychologically, in my memory. From that unconventional audience with Mrs Bogart I kept my appointment with Gerry who went on to oblige me with a goal against Ipswich the following day. I didn't keep a record of my article about him – though I don't fancy *To Have and Have Not* warranted even a passing mention.

THE SOCCER STAR WHO SHUNNED THE BIG TIME

Western Daily Press, 1977

He played his last game of football exactly 50 years ago – and they still talk about him in the Somerset town where he was born and became the idol.

He is extolled in the way that others extol timeless international stars like Puskas and Pele. The first division clubs held out their tempting inducements. Tottenham, in particular, pleaded with him to join them. They could have turned him into an England player. But he chose to stay with humble Yeovil for 20 years. In that time he scored 548 goals.

His presence on the quaint, sloping Huish ground was guaranteed to excite every soccer fan in South Somerset. He was a gentle, diffident centre forward, uncoached and uncomplicated in his approach to association football. But he had magnetic natural skill and charisma like no Yeovil player before or since. His name: Fred (Johnny) Hayward.

And the question they still ask in the town is why he never left his modest job in the gloving industry to sample first division football. One of his two sons, Cyril Hayward, too young ever to have seen Johnny play, admits there were private regrets from his father in later life that he did not sample league soccer. "Dad would watch it on television, and I could see what was going through his mind. I think perhaps he felt he didn't make the most of his ability."

There was certainly parental opposition, too. One relative told me: "I don't think Johnny's father ever watched him play. On the one occasion when he walked to the ground, the opposition failed to turn up."

Cyril has a watch given to Johnny by his parents in an attempt to influence his decision to stay at home. And home was important to the quiet-spoken, good-living Johnny. He was happiest of all when surrounded by his family. It was quite a number – seven daughters and two sons.

He was at heart an amateur. There were many county appearances for Somerset. He often recalled with genuine affection his early games for Yeovil Baptists and the Boys' Brigade. Only in the last few years with Yeovil & Petters United, as the club was then called, did he receive any money. He was rather embarrassed about taking it.

A nephew said: "He was never a professional footballer in spirit. It was only that professionalism overtook the club."

Not that the bonuses were likely to make you rich. It was five shillings for a win and half a crown for a draw. The soccer wages went straight into the family budget.

Johnny played in every forward position except outside right. He was born in Wellington Street, just round the corner from the Huish ground, and played his first game for Yeovil in 1907. By 1921, he was knocking in 60 goals a season. Mainly with his left foot. The Hayward left foot was legendary, in fact.

My father watched him in home games and idolised him like every other young lad in his cloth cap on the terraces. He said: "Whenever you saw him brace his left foot, you knew it was a goal. It was lethal."

Arthur Riggs, president of the First Yeovil Company Boys' Brigade, knew Johnny for years. "He was a very nice person in every way, and I never remember him committing a foul."

Yet what was so special about him? Why did first division scouts from all over the country come to the small market town to see this shy glove-sorter run out in his green and white shirt on a Saturday afternoon? "He had it all – and what a shot," says Percy May, the full back of those days, who still lives in Yeovil.

But, in truth, Johnny was not the all-round footballer. He was not exceptionally fast. Not many of his goals came from headers. Some even called him one-footed. Bill Garrett, of Somerton, watched him "hundreds of times, right back in his Pen Mills days". And he's in no doubt about the one magical skill that made Johnny Hayward a great footballer. "It was his swerve. He left defenders standing. I have never seen a better body-swerve on the field."

For 20 years he enthralled Yeovil crowds and consistently frustrated league managers. He even went out in style. His last game was against Lovells Athletic. And he scored seven goals.

Johnny left others to do the talking and to ponder on why he stayed in Somerset. He died aged 71, but not before he had seen his two sons, Ken and Cyril, briefly play for Yeovil.

Half a century after he kicked his last ball for the local team he chose in preference to Spurs, the Huish supporters – even those who were not born when he played – still talk ecstatically about him.

West Country sport has never had a more unassuming and unlikely hero.

MY NIGHT IN A DOSS HOUSE

Bristol Evening Post, 1970

*This is one of many features I wrote that contained social comment.
This night of disturbed sleep at Cheltenham saw me, stubble and all,
among the nomadic drunks. I always tried to avoid phoney 'play acting'
as I searched for authenticity.*

Midnight in the dosshouse. I'm in the corner bed, lying in my socks and two sweaters. It's freezing outside. The naked bulbs have been switched off for nearly an hour. I curl in a ball, gaze unseeingly into the darkness … and listen.

There are the snores and the groans, the incessant coughing and the spitting into the chamber-pots. And the snatches of conversation from all corners of the dormitory: "P.J. … Here, P.J. I'm off next week. You can have my bed next week, P.J."

"You've been trying hard, Brummie."

"Yea, got a job at Lichfield. Sounds all right. Kitchen porter and nine quid a week."

And then silence again. You hear a hopeful banging on the door downstairs. But someone is going to be unlucky. All the 53 beds at Rowton House, Cheltenham, are taken. Several late-comers are already kipping on a battered settee. It's a bitter night and the coughing goes on. And the curses. "My bloody chest is done for. It needs the doctor."

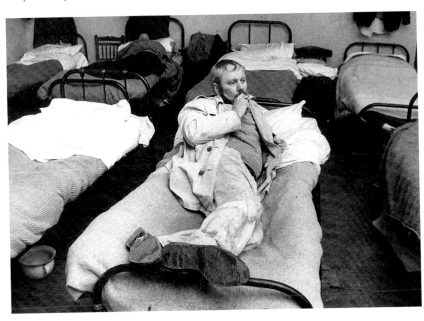

Hard to associate this with 1970. Hard to associate it with Regency Cheltenham, where the Young Ladies get the right education and the fashionable Promenade symbolises affluence.

The beds are only a few feet apart. Each with its polythene sheeting as a precaution against bed-wetting; each with its pot underneath. There is no furniture and no lockers. Your trousers are slung under the pillow; you don't take your shirt off.

"Hey, what about Cassius then? He proved to the world, boy, that he's a religious man. It was his religion that done it …"

The voice was unmistakably Irish. Good Catholic sentiments in the doss-house at midnight. There are plenty of Irishmen around me: Noonan and Connolly and Daly and "Corky" and two P.J.s (Patrick Joseph).

They pay 7s 6d a night (less for the week) for the bed. They cook their food on a gas stove and they crowd avidly round a big wooden table in the evening to watch the telly on a flickering set. It's a luxury that provides the only diversion from lying on the bed or nattering in the communal kitchen.

But they don't talk a lot. When I arrived in early evening, they were watching telly in darkness. Twenty or so of them sitting silently, like indeterminate eerie statues, looking at an old film about cosy family life. The occasional grunt was the only communication during the film. But they laughed at the commercial about the good strong beer that followed.

Three-quarters of them are regulars at Rowton House. Some have come in from the cold. They shuffle along to the kitchen after the telly and suddenly the little cardboard boxes magically appear, with their irons, their packet of marge and raw onions. It's supper time.

A friendly Scot passes me a mug of strong tea. I finger my week's stubble self-consciously and hope he won't ask me where I'm from. We get on to jobs and I'm assured that Cheltenham is no good – "there's nothing down the Labour."

It's a strangely silent institution. When they talk, the accents are thick and the laughter sparse. But there is a dry humour of a sort in the wash-house where someone has crudely converted a notice into what might be a Limerick racecard.

… It's now the early hours and I stay awake listening to the coughing. And I think of the words of Mary Priday, a warm-hearted woman who with her husband looks after the lodging house: "They're a good lot of lads, really. Perhaps they like a drink at the week-end but there isn't much trouble. If I see them getting a bit naughty down at the pub, I just look at them and say don't let the House down. It usually works." Of the bed-wetting, she says: "What can you expect? Some of them have been sleeping rough. They catch a cold in their kidneys. They can't help themselves."

Christmas at Rowton House will again be a bed for the night. But there will be a special tea laid out on that big bare table. "I've got the lads to pick up blue stamps when they've bought their food at the Co-op. The stamps are worth £5 and this will go towards the tea. It's no point getting anything special for dinner. Some of them will be having a drink and they'll just want to sleep when they get back."

Rowton House is, in the main, a home for the homeless. If there were more beds they could be filled. If there were more money, the basic facilities could be improved. "We're desperately short of cash," says Ald. Charles Irving, chairman of the South West Midlands Housing Society who bought the dilapidated building to make sure the Rowton occupants would still have a roof for the night.

… Long before six in the morning and Brummie is beginning to tell us of his new job again. He's a nice bloke and everyone is glad for him. P.J. will get his bed. No one really knows the time but it's just the start of another day. And every day is roughly about the same as the last there.

But thank goodness, I think to myself, that there is a Rowton House at all.

PUNCH-DRUNK AND LED TO THE GALLOWS

Bristol Evening Post, 2007

> *The pacifist in me clashed on occasions with the strident excitement of the primeval prize fight. I knew and liked some of the local boxers, and I also queued for an hour to collect Tommy Farr's autograph. I warmed to the skeletal fighters who between the first and second world wars took on three opponents a night at a fiver a time. That was working-class glamour, raw and not always well supervised or handled with enough medical care. In Bristol one 14-year-old boxer, Jimmy Cooper, died in the ring.*

In the 1920s and '30s, pale, lean boxers, ever grateful for an extra fiver, frantically took on as many bouts as they could find. Medical supervision was minimal. Little Tosh Parker once fought three times a day during the miners' strike.

Some of the better fights were at venues like the prestigious Colston Hall. Others were in more modest boxing halls or transformed pub sheds. Every fight night bulged with fans – and every supporter had his favourite.

Del Fontaine was one – a French Canadian who had come over in a cattle boat with the intention of establishing himself as a fighter. His style in the ring was all-action. The trouble was that he had little or no defence. He took a battering in almost every contest but invariably grinned at the crowd as he stumbled back, bruised and beaten, to an improvised dressing room.

Del Fontaine wasn't his real name – it was really Raymond Henry Bousquet, a name too long to fit the billboards. But from the bell, his fists flailing, he was marvellous value. Sadly, even his most loyal fans came to realise that he was on the slide. By 1934, he had lost 12 of his last 14 bouts. Those closest to him suspected that he was becoming punch-drunk.

He was a colourful personality – his dashing looks made him especially popular with Bristol girls. He also liked a drink. Back in Canada, he had a wife and children.

Between fights, however, he spent more and more time with a pretty 21-year-old waitress, Hilda Meek, born in the city's Winstanley Street. The relationship became increasingly obsessional. Hilda, described by her friends as flighty, had no wish to be tied down – especially by a moody prize-fighter whose face and body were increasingly showing the bruises and effects of his last bout.

One day he heard her making a date with another man. The neurotic Fontaine suddenly pulled out a gun and fired – she died on the spot. Another shot injured her mother.

176

Del Fontaine

The West Country sporting public was shocked. At the trial, which as a crime of passion fired the nation, the defence called on welterweight champion Ted Lewis. He looked across the courtroom at the crumpled, demoralised Fontaine and spluttered emotionally: "Del shouldn't have been in the ring at all for his last fight. He wasn't in a fit state. As a boxer, he has received more punishment than anyone I have ever seen."

The verdict was inevitable. Not that Hilda's distraught father helped the boxer's case. Sam Meek, of Barton Hill, was questioned about Fontaine's state of mental health. "Do you realise that he was knocked out seven times recently?" The reply was bitterly cynical, devoid of any affection: "I don't know about knock-outs. The last one seemed to me like a lie-down."

The implication was that, by then, Del Fontaine, aware that any slender hopes of progressing in the ring had disappeared, was prepared to take a dive. It would have been the ultimate insult to a boxer so often acclaimed by Bristol crowds for his crash-bang approach.

By the time the date for the execution had been decided, the protests had started. They grew in volume as Fontaine's friends pleaded for a reprieve. There were long lists of names on the petitions, asking for his life to be spared. How could the judiciary send a punch-drunk, deeply depressed man of unsound mind to the gallows?

But it did. Outside the prison gates, on the morning of the execution, religious figures led the hymns. Politicians made intense anti-capital punishment speeches. It made no difference. The prison bell tolled and the weeping crowds, including a few familiar faces from the world of boxing, strolled away.

Del Fontaine left a note. "Hilda Meek broke my heart. I spent my last cent on her. She turned me against my own wife."

Al Harding, of the well-known local boxing family – he had persuaded Del to come to the West Country, and another brother, Percy, had been a promoter at the Gem Stadium – cycled to London to see Fontaine in the condemned cell. For two outwardly tough characters, it had been a tearful experience.

Back in Bristol, amid hoarse cheers and the Woodbine-fuggy atmosphere, the boxing shows went on – sluggers searching for unattainable glory. At the Gem, that popular venue in Broad Weir, the fans continued to argue over the fate of the swarthy French-Canadian they had all taken to their hearts. From the Gem to the gallows had been a short, poignant journey.

After the hanging, the wardens whispered to visitor Harding: "He was the bravest bloke we ever saw go to the gallows."

It was the human quality Del demonstrated with such unfulfilled and misdirected zeal in the ring.

SOFTLY SOFTLY

Western Daily Press, 2006

Softly Softly was my favourite cop show on television back in the Sixties and Seventies. It was tightly written, abrasive and character-based, a long way on from dear old PC Dixon who used to patrol the streets of Dock Green with paternal bonhomie. The series was a spin-off of that gritty, ground-breaking *Z Cars*, introduced by the creative Troy Kennedy Martin. With its social realism and Merseyside story-lines, police cars, sirens blazing and occupants arguing, splashed through grimy inner-city byways in search of the villains – and, much to the horror of the real police, these cops' private lives could be pretty grimy, too.

Softly Softly kept together the two senior officers from *Z Cars*, played by Stratford Johns and Frank Windsor, and it is true to say I was addicted to this new show, which was mostly produced in Bristol and filmed in the West Country. I persuaded myself that there was only one way to see the series at close quarters – and that was by being in it. Astonishingly, I managed to appear in a dozen episodes.

In truth, it may have been hard to spot me. I was an extra, paid a not inconsiderable six guineas a day and not allowed – whatever the temptation to offer a pearl of throwaway dialogue – to utter a single word in the presence of the nearest camera or microphone.

That I made any appearance at all is not easy to explain. Professionally I had no obvious thespian aspirations and was not a member of Equity, the actors' trade union and one more militant than most at that time in succeeding to keep non-members at bay.

But *Softly Softly* had logistical problems. It had a pool of extras it could call on, but many lived well away from Bristol. The episodes were filmed on a tight schedule and the need to find someone at the last minute was a constant challenge for the casting people. At the time I was working part-time in the BBC newsroom, so I picked up on the gossip as I eavesdropped on actors in the canteen.

Needing to supplement my meagre freelance wages in those days, I presumptuously applied for an occasional role, however nominal, alongside my heroes – Stratford Johns as Detective Chief Superintendent Charlie Barlow, his quieter, contrasting sidekick Frank Windsor as John Watt, and Norman Bowler, who as Sergeant Harry Hawkins had already acquired a very passable West Country accent.

My cheeky application led to an interview. "But you aren't Equity, are you?" "Erm, well, no." Long pause. "Do you belong to any union?" "The National Union of Journalists."

There was another long delay as the casting woman looked anxiously down her list. "Maybe we can swing it. But don't mention it to anyone else. It's not something Equity approves of. You'd better turn up at eight o'clock in the morning. The coach will be waiting here in Whiteladies Road."

I was there – then and for 11 more episodes. On the first day of filming, the director liked to line up the extras and assess how best they could be used. My craggy, slightly dissipated features apparently lent themselves to sleazy lawlessness.

I was a crook four or five times. Shady, salacious … and silent. I also played a gormless copper, a police photographer – with a flash camera I struggled to operate – on hand when a body was pulled out of the Avon in Bristol's Hotwells, and as an observant bystander.

There was a commendable versatility about my work. Frank Windsor once complimented me. Norman Bowler, whom I got on well with between takes, told me he was coming to Bristol to live, and so he did for many years. I stuck to my instructions and didn't reveal my non-luvvie pedigree.

This was not my most embarrassing experience. That happened when we were filming in a field at Dundry, Somerset. I was a young detective and my job was to capture and arrest a villain making good his escape. Ironically, he was being played by a mate of mine in the BBC newsroom, an illustrator for *Points West* called Peter Andrews, who happened to be an ex-actor and really did have an Equity card.

One of the lessons I learned during my flirtation with BBC Drama was to be wary of young directors on the make. The one orchestrating the fisticuffs in that Dundry field liked rough physical action. "I want this to be a realistic scrap and I'm going to let it run," he said. "Your job is to pitch into Peter. Fists, the lot. But it won't be as hairy as it looks. I'm going to tell him not to resist you, just appear to." He then spoke privately to my workmate-turned-opponent. He told him exactly the same – to give me a thoroughly bad time, but I wouldn't be resisting. It was a crafty and unforgivable move. The fight was for real and lasted for ages. Neither Peter nor I was quite sure what was going on. I suffered a bruised cheek and my raincoat – my own raincoat – was badly torn.

"Great bout," the director said. "I'll feature it." He didn't seem to hear my protests about a coat I wouldn't be able to wear again.

Softly Softly was a success – for the quality of its writing, the feuding among the coppers, the breathless tracking of the criminals. South African Stratford Johns was an on-screen bully, admired as an actor and hated by viewers for his aggressive style, but when the cameras weren't running, he seemed to get on well with the more sensitive Frank Windsor.

In fact we all got on well – in my case, because no one ever discovered that I was just a fan living a dream.

MY FAVOURITE CRICKETER – ARTHUR WELLARD

The Wisden Cricketer, 2007

To someone embedded so incorrigibly in the ways, wonders and human oddities of West Country cricket over the decades the choice was one of wavering loyalties. It could have been Harold Gimblett for those instinctive, understated skills, Horace 'Nutty' Hazell for his jovial demeanour and evocative portly waistline, Reg Sinfield for his Tommy Trinder chin and battered boxer's nose or Bill Andrews, so often my confidant, who gave me gossip without a trace of malice. My affection was unbounded. But in the end I went for Arthur Wellard.

The earliest impressions never go away. I still see him strolling off the field at my hometown ground at Yeovil in the late 1930s when Lancashire were the visitors. Winston Place and Eddie Paynter, names vaguely familiar to me, were playing but I did not notice them. It was Wellard I wanted to see up close. I ran across to the modest pavilion at the close of play. He was tall, manly, his dark hair greased back around the central parting, thick, bronzed arms around the neck of a team-mate half his size. What a cricketer, I decided. I already knew he hit sixes and took wickets for a living.

That was my first sight of him. The second, again at a Yeovil ground, was at a Sunday benefit match. In the tea interval I anonymously patrolled the surrounds, in the hope of a fleeting moment of doting proximity. Then suddenly here he was, approaching me. No one else about. If only he would say: "Hello, son, enjoying the cricket?" Anything, in fact. What he did say was: "Hey son, where's the bogs round hure?"

It was not the most romantic of conversational gambits. I stammered a response and pointed in the right direction. He thanked me and was on his way, no doubt to dispose of a little of the pre-match cheer. The voice, I discovered, carried the suggestion of regional vowels, acquired over the past ten years or so after Kent had been tardy about signing him and Somerset found him digs in Weston-super-Mare.

Wellard was one of Somerset's greatest bowlers and only Farmer White took more wickets for them. He played in two Tests and would have gone to India in 1939 but for the war. My schoolboy contemporaries, like me, loved to ape his leap in the delivery stride. We collected the action pictures and chuckled over the way he seemed occasionally to tuck his left arm behind him at the same time as if scratching his back. In fact the action was orthodox. He consistently swung the ball away from the right-handers; his break-backs were renowned. Many of his wickets came when he clean-bowled startled batsmen – just as well perhaps; too many catches went down ritualistically in the slips from the county's successive clutches of transitory amateurs.

Arthur Wellard

When, after the war, the limbs ached more, he turned to off-spin. There was still native cunning: after he had surreptitiously brought in another slip he would unexpectedly let go an old-style seamer. His fielding, full of sang-froid, was at times as comical as it was intrepid. On hot days he took out his teeth when stationed at silly mid-off. It changed his appearance considerably and, according to several of the pros, his improvised dentistry bordered on gamesmanship.

One of the county scorers worked out that a quarter of Wellard's runs came from sixes. He dispensed entertainment and there were groans when he was quickly out, not just from West Country crowds. His routine was to play back the first half a dozen deliveries with mannered coaching-school correctness. After that, whether the bowling was fast or slow, he aimed for the clouds. A succession of coaches encouraged him to hit straighter. Mostly they let him get on with it.

Arthur, one felt, should have been a jokey extrovert. In fact, he was surprisingly laconic. The voice, when not inclining to Taunton and the

Blackdowns, was more cockney than Man of Kent. "Come in a bit at cover, cock," he would say. Everyone was "cock". He got animated only when he went racing. That was something he did perhaps a little too often on a Somerset pro's frugal salary.

Andrews idolised him "even though he always bowled with the wind behind him and I suffered at the other end." When the newcomer arrived from Kent, Bill was in awe of his appearance: his gaudy ties, check sports coats and pointed shoes. Not that Wellard was flashy but he carried an aura of self-contained sophistication. Yet he was basically an uncomplicated man. When it rained, he produced a pack of cards. He left the majority of the professionals, fledglings when it came to poker – or, more often, brag – out of pocket. Bill used to say: "He could remember the position of every card in the pack – he was out of our class."

So he was in most cases when it came to cricket. In his first season for the county he took 131 wickets. Three times he did the double. Twice at Wells he belted five sixes in an over, scattering the dreamy young theological students seated at long-on. Oldies claim he could hit the ball farther than Guy Earle and even Viv Richards. Those who saw his hundreds at The Oval and Old Trafford would agree.

Everyone liked Arthur. That included Harold Pinter who wrote affectionately about him and probably considered it a coup when Wellard agreed to play on occasions for the playwright's XI. Like most of my fellow Somerset friends I was outraged when Somerset chose in 1950 not to re-engage him.

WHEN DAD MET TS ELIOT

Guardian, 2008

Lloyd George knew my father. Well, not quite true – it was TS Eliot who knew my father. Or perhaps in my search for absolute veracity, literary or otherwise, it should be admitted that the acquaintanceship lasted for no more than ten minutes.

Eliot had, in the late thirties, come to the Somerset village of East Coker for almost the only time, visiting the church as a precursor to the publication in 1940 of his *Four Quartets*, one of which concerned itself with the parish's Hamstone charm and high protective grassy banks as well as the hidden meanings that academics continue to ponder.

He was not, as far as I know, a sporting man. His upbringing had been in the United States and one assumes that the wondrous deeds of Hobbs and Hammond made little or no impact on his cerebral imagery. Certainly he did not go around, like AE Housman for instance, in casual wear and a cricket cap. His clothes were more cut for sedentary use than for loping round the boundary.

On that summer's evening he arrived and sat in a pew behind the font. His was an unfamiliar face and my father, who earned £5 a quarter as St Michael's sexton, responsible for cutting the grass between the tombstones, keeping possession of the keys to the tower's spiral staircase and trimming the wicks of the hanging oil lamps, readily engaged the newcomer in amiable conversation.

I have no idea how easy and balanced the exchanges were but am sure that Dad, as usual, wasted no time in offering a comprehensive who's who of local players, cricketers and footballers, and a glossary of their varying skills. There was Tommy Hackwell, who looked like Chaplin, the village undertaker who carved coffins every bit as neatly as he fashioned his punctilious strokes; Roy Haines – "a proper wicketkeeper every bit as good as Ames"; and Cockles Stevens, reserve goalkeeper for Yeovil, who doubled up by reading the lesson at matins.

Cockles, renowned for the depth of his goal-kicks, used to give us the scriptures in a rural voice of sonorous authority, almost as if he was demanding a back-pass from his full-back. My father reasoned that the goalkeeper's familiarity with the Bible was a spiritual titbit worth throwing in.

The parental report, relayed over supper, did not indicate what sort of feedback he got. But he was much impressed with the pious bearing of the man sitting behind the font. "Seemed a nice kind of bloke. Quite religious, you could tell." A few days later the vicar told Dad he knew the visitor had wanted a look at the church. A bit of a writer.

TS Eliot apparently loved the village but never returned (though his ashes did). As far as we know, the knowledge he gleaned about Cockles' goalkeeping and Roy's stumpings did not find their way into the poet's abstruse wasteland. Dad did not go in for flights of word-music but he always liked the chance of a chat with strangers. He would put down his can of paraffin to volunteer an unsolicited run-down of local sportsmen's achievements. It always seemed to him a perfectly natural form of discussion.

It is possible he forgot to mention Charlie Mayo. That would have been a pity. Charlie was the only Old Etonian to play for East Coker Cricket Club. He was talented enough to play half a dozen times for the county. It would have been more but he was killed in action. He had lived across the road from me and encouraged me to play cricket. Eliot would have been more interested in the pet raven, which travelled miles on Charlie's shoulder. The bird's one felony, demanding a Freudian explanation, was to steal women's underwear from clothes lines.

In those dreamy days the village had a fine cricket ground, the outfield lush from the excretal habits of farmer Denning's sheep. The fixture list was suitably ambitious, including visits from old-school XIs complete with their funny double-barrelled members' names. County amateurs, resplendent in their flannels and kaleidoscopic blazers, were always playing for or against East Coker. Sydney Rippon, father of Geoffrey, QC and MP, who created a stir by once playing for Somerset under his grandmother's name because he was on sick leave, would have preferred the calm at East Coker to the complications and in his case, subterfuge, of first-class sport.

It was this quiet that Eliot also liked. Sadly, we have to assume, cricket and football did not come into it.

FARM LABOURER – OR CREATIVE GENIUS?

from the book 'West Country Mysteries', 1985

'Wold Tommy Shayell', as they called him in south Somerset, died more than a hundred and fifty years ago. But a few of the older villagers at Montacute, stirred by the stories about him passed on by succeeding generations of their own families, still pretend that they can remember him.

The tragedy was that Tommy – christened Thomas Shoel – met with none of the deserved recognition during his lifetime, the kind that would have fed and kept alive his careworn, undernourished wife and children.

He was a composer and a poet. And yet he was never taught a note of music and had virtually no schooling. If only he'd been born in a fashionable city and found the right patrons, the critics would have extolled his work and he would have been acclaimed nationally. He would also have been given the added education, to complement his exceptional natural talents and sensitivity.

In Montacute and the neighbouring parishes nestling at the foot of Ham Hill, his contemporaries shook their heads. They watched him composing his verse or his hymn tunes as he sat astride a stile or sprawled contemplatively in the grass. They couldn't understand his poems and had no especial regard for the esoteric mood of church music. But at the same time they marvelled at the pastoral metaphors that he created, the notes that he scored with such melodic ability.

"Where do Tommy get it from? He bain't like the rest of us. He bides for hours up on Ham Hill," they used to say.

The local clergy were rather more forthcoming with their theories. "Thomas is inspired from above," they assured their flocks.

'Wold Tommy' was in many ways an unlikely candidate for divine gifts. He had the voice and the appearance of a simple villager who knew his place in life: and in Montacute that meant unrelenting labours bound by the feudal strictures of the time. No-one could ever remember him going to school. He worked as a farm labourer and a village carter. His health was bad. His face was drawn and his shoulders stooped in the way of most villagers who eked out a living. Yet if he had a sickle in one hand, there was invariably a stub of lead pencil in the other. He was different.

Tom Shoel was born in 1759. His parents died when he was still a small boy. He grew up in acute poverty and was learning to 'hedge and ditch' of necessity almost from the moment he could walk. It was assumed that his life would be as hard, mundane and unfulfilled as other boys of his age in Montacute.

But he grew up 'with music in me head'. He was given a tin whistle and the tunes multiplied. He went to church and learned to read from the Bible. The old vicars to whom he listened entranced were really his only school teachers. Laboriously he taught himself to write. The letters were beautifully formed; the incongruous farm-worker gripped the pencil in his rough-grained fingers and produced copperplate.

He may have been eccentric in some of his behaviour and spent hours on his own wandering the lanes of Stoke-sum-Hamdon, Chiselborough and the Chinnocks. At the same time he longed for the relative convention of a family life. He married a local girl and soon had several children. Their poverty, not unusual in those times among rural communities, was appalling. Child-bearing weakened an already prematurely frail young woman. His wife died; so in the next few years did all the children with the exception of one son.

Tom was distraught. He was left with only his prayers and his 'inner music'. The prayers intensified. The music took on a melancholic element. His emerging poems assumed a surprisingly mature philosophic character.

In his late thirties he married again. There were three more children, all daughters. The collective prayers didn't fill their stomachs. His wife had twins when she was 49. The unequal struggle was eventually too much for her and she killed herself. Her husband was again overcome by grief. "Better fit he do a bit mer work and fergit his writin'," the villagers were apt to say, as if blaming him for the succession of family tragedies.

But Tom couldn't adjust to such harrowing realities. Was he a romantic – or a near genius? Or something of both?

He'd given up all but the token amount of local labouring to buy a loaf or two of bread. His hymn tunes were becoming more prolific. And so were his poems. They were meticulously copied out in his copperplate. A kindly clergyman arranged for three books of his sacred music and several slim volumes of his poems to be published in Bristol. They made him little if any money.

He became more unconventional in his habits. He never touched meat, even if he could have afforded it. He talked away to himself, and even those who didn't understand him realised that here was a rare and extraordinary talent.

Tom became 'an instant composer'. When the brass band arrived for a special performance on an annual festival after Trinity Sunday, they discovered that they didn't have their music with them. "Wold Tommy'll do summick for thee," they were told. And so he did. He sat down on a barrel of beer in the yard of the Phelips Arms, according to the late Llewellyn Powys in one of his lovely evocative essays, and composed a new tune for the band. More than that, he scored it for each different instrument. Such a feat of spontaneous creativity was worth sixpence to him. He seldom earned more than half that for one of his hymns.

Thomas Shoel peddled his tunes. He was a hymnsmith who then set off to try to sell his compositions. Occasionally when he headed for Bristol, he would be lucky enough to hitch a lift part of the way on a stage waggon. Often his speculative sorties, with the new hymn in the pocket of his ragged coat, would take him several days. He slept rough on the way, living off turnips and swedes. But there was never a guarantee of a threepenny sale at the end of the journey.

There were many times in earlier years when he penned an anthem or a poem in great haste hopefully to earn a few pence to buy food for one of his sick children. Life never got easier for him.

A few people sensed his rare gifts. He had neither the resources nor the physique to parade his talents before wider audiences. To their everlasting shame, one or two literary figures to whom his work was sent by kindly regional well-wishers hardly bothered to read or assess it.

What could an illiterate farm labourer from a Somerset village know about choral music or literature? If they had only taken the trouble to encourage him, they would have been rewarded. One critic took a look at Tom's poetry and implied that it must have been plagiarised. No 'hedger and ditcher' could have dreamed up those words or had those ethereal thoughts.

Wold Tommy was influenced by no-one save the God he heard about in church. He educated himself – and strolled the country lanes and hillsides to put his thoughts, all spiritually based, onto paper.

What did it matter that the spelling was bad, the construction amd metre naïve and the occasional word misused?

He died in 1823 and they took his body to a burial place called Five Ashes, on the outskirts of nearby Odcombe and just along the narrow winding lane from his beloved Ham Hill. Five Acres is an acre of consecrated ground, oddly located in the middle of pasture-land. It is guarded by a high wall, originally built to keep the body-snatchers away. Today the burial place is deserted and overgrown. Here lies Thomas Shoel and some of his family. The names on the leaning tombstones can no longer be read.

He was a remarkable man. He wrote hundreds of poems and hymns. Many of them died with him, unread and unappreciated. We shall never know how near he was to minor genius. A few scholars who came after him studied snatches of his poems and were glowing in their praise. They only regretted that much of his work was lost.

Villagers who grew up with him at Montacute were apt to scoff at his preoccupied demeanour. Others could only wonder at his sheer output – and the depth of thought and sensitivity of a man who never went to school.

Given his background and the abject poverty that dogged him, there can have been few creative accomplishments within the West country to equal Wold Tommy's. His prodigious talents seemed to be manifested without effort or the agonised gestations that so often characterise imaginative outpourings. Till this day, his inspired work remains an absorbing mystery.

Could those erstwhile Montacute churchmen have been right when they pointed to his simple, undeviating faith and said: "He gets it from above."

Five Ashes burial ground

INDEX

David Foot and his family are not included